Henry James achieved a transient popularity with some of his early tales of Americans in Europe; thereafter, as his writing grew more intense and highly wrought, contemporary readers mainly failed to appreciate what he was doing. Since his death nearly sixty years ago, it has come to be recognised that the quality and volume of what he achieved place him among the greatest practitioners of the art of fiction.

The first chapter of this study traces some of the main events of James's life, outwardly a quiet one like those of his heroes and heroines, but momentous for the range of observation recorded and experience digested in America, England, France and Italy. Mr. Pirie shows how well placed James was to take an informed critical view of the 'mixture of manners' in the modern Western world which has resulted largely from factors that conditioned his own upbringing to an unusual degree: increasing affluence, easier travel, and the relaxing of old principles and constraints.

Mr. Pirie then chooses five novels and two tales for detailed study. Between them, they show the variety of James's achievement in fiction, from the small domestic canvas of *Washington Square* to the large international one of *The Portrait of a Lady,* from the gentle pastoral comedy of *The Europeans* to the hilarious satire of urban life in *The Bostonians.* No fixed method of explication is followed, but Mr. Pirie has attempted to show what each work is about, how James developed a narrative technique adequate to express the fine moral sensibility with which he endows his characters, and how that technique gives his work its peculiar elegance and intensity. The last chapter summarises some of those features that distinguish James's work both as a representation of the real world, and as a visionary world with a special coherence of its own.

Literature in Perspective

General Editor: Kenneth Grose

Henry James

Literature in Perspective

Henry James

Gordon Pirie

Rowman and Littlefield, Totowa, N. J.

First published in the United States, 1975
by Rowman and Littlefield, Totowa, New Jersey

© Gordon Pirie 1974

ISBN 0–87471–611–x

Printed in Great Britain

Literature in Perspective

Reading is a pleasure; reading great literature is a great pleasure, which can be enhanced by increased understanding, both of the actual words on the page and of the background to those words, supplied by a study of the author's life and circumstances. Criticism should try to foster understanding in both aspects.

Unfortunately for the intelligent layman and young reader alike, recent years have seen critics of literature (particularly academic ones) exploring slender ramifications of meaning, exposing successive levels of association and reference, and multiplying the types of ambiguity unto seventy times seven.

But a poet is 'a man speaking to men', and the critic should direct his efforts to explaining not only what the poet says, but also what sort of man the poet is. It is our belief that it is impossible to do the first without doing the second.

Literature in Perspective, therefore, aims at giving a straightforward account of literature and of writers—straightforward both in content and in language. Critical jargon is as far as possible avoided; any terms that must be used are explained simply; and the constant preoccupation of the authors of the series is to be lucid.

It is our hope that each book will be easily understood, that it will adequately describe its subject without pretentiousness so that the intelligent reader who wants to know about Donne or Keats or Shakespeare will find enough in it to bring him up to date on critical estimates.

Even those who are well read, we believe, can benefit from a lucid exposition of what they may have taken for granted, and perhaps—dare it be said?—not fully understood.

K. H. G.

Henry James

During the fifty years of his working life, Henry James published some sixty volumes of prose. Pre-eminently, these include twenty novels and over one hundred stories, but also literary criticism, plays, biography, autobiography and topographical essays. This is a large achievement by any standards, and by his standards, which were extremely fastidious, it is monumental. Little that he wrote can be dismissed as second-rate, and none of it is without interest. It follows that my subject vastly exceeds the scope of this study, and my treatment has been arbitrarily selective.

The first chapter deals with James's life, and glances briefly at some aspects of his work on which it seemed the life had some light to throw. Chapters 2–6, the bulk of the book, discuss five novels in some detail. These five were not chosen with any conviction that they represent the best of James. The choice reflects to some extent my own preference; but if it includes only one of the late works, that is not because I prefer the early ones, but because this is supposed to be a critical introduction for those coming new to James, and the early works offer an easier foothold. There are at least six other novels—*The Princess Casamassima*, *The Tragic Muse*, *The Awkward Age*, *The Ambassadors*, *The Wings of the Dove* and *The Golden Bowl*—that have as good a claim to be called major works as any of my chosen five. Regretfully, I have devoted only one chapter to the short stories, or tales, the twelve volumes of which would merit a separate study. I have said even less about the large and distinguished body of James's non-fictional works, among which the following seem to me outstanding: the criticism of other writers, notably his fellow-novelists both French and English; the topographical essays, gathered in such volumes as *Portraits of Places*, *English Hours*, *Italian Hours* and *The American Scene*; and the autobiography, from which I have quoted repeatedly in Chapter 1.

I am indebted to several colleagues for their advice and encouragement: above all to Ken Grose, the General Editor of this series, but also to John Thorn, my headmaster, for giving me the chance to get started, and to Leslie Russon, Jack Blakiston, Kenneth Kettle and David Smith. I am also grateful to my family for putting up with the back view of composition.

The page references for quotations from the novels are to the current Penguin editions. R. G. P.

Acknowledgements

The author and publishers are indebted to the National Gallery for the use of the cover portrait.

Contents

The Author

Gordon Pirie was Head of the Department of English at Winchester College.

I

The Life (1843–1916)

A major figure in both English and American literature, Henry James was the first great writer to belong to both sides of the Atlantic. A brief outline of the movements of his life will show that he was a cosmopolitan by upbringing before he became one by choice.

He was born in New York in 1843, the second son of wealthy American parents who promptly took him and his brother to Europe for two years. His first memory was of the Place Vendôme in Paris. The 'poison' of Europe, as he later put it, thus entered early into his veins. The family, now four sons and a daughter, were back in New York and New England until Henry was twelve; but by this time the father, who could afford such speculation, was wondering whether America offered the best opportunities for his children: 'We gravely ponder whether it would not be better to go abroad for a few years with them, allowing them to absorb French and German and get a better sensuous education than they are likely to get here.' So they went for three years to England, France and Switzerland, and sampled a variety of schools and tutors. Then they came back to America—'I have no doubt,' wrote the father, 'that our own schools are much superior to the European schools.' But a year later, with the father now 'so discouraged about the education of my children here', they took ship again for a further twelve months in Europe. These wanderings covered the years of Henry's adolescence. Then the parents settled down in New England, and from the age of seventeen he was at home there for nine years. In 1869 he went alone to Europe for a year of energetic exploration and passionate appreciation. Thereafter,

America seemed less and less possible as a home for the young writer. He escaped again to Europe in 1872 for two years, spent mostly in Italy. After another attempt to settle down in America he crossed again in 1875 and tried Paris. 'If one can't be in London, this is next best.' A year later he *was* in London, and for the next forty years England was his home. Yet he continued to visit America, published his work there and in England concurrently, went on to the end of his career writing about Americans at home and abroad, and renounced his American citizenship only when the First World War brought home to him how deeply his affections were engaged in the fortunes of England.

The genuinely cosmopolitan novelist is a rarity. Earlier novelists had travelled, and written briefly of foreign places in their fiction, but in his stories of Americans in Europe James was the first to write great fiction with a foreign setting, foreign both to himself and his characters, and in his middle period he was the first to make another country sufficiently his own to depict it wholly from within: English characters in an English setting. Why did America become impossible for him as a home and inadequate as a subject, and why was it finally England where he settled, and not France or Italy? To answer these questions we must first consider the remarkable family that produced him.

Henry James Senior, father of the novelist, was the son of an Irish immigrant who made a fortune in business, had thirteen children and was a pillar of the Presbyterian Church. Left a man of leisure on his father's death, he set himself to study theology. Reacting against a strict Calvinist upbringing, he found in Emanuel Swedenborg, the Swedish theologian, a God of Love to replace the fierce Calvinist deity. Under the influence of Swedenborg and of Charles Fourier, the French social reformer, he devoted his life to elaborating a new, liberal conception of God and of man's relation to Him. 'Every appetite and passion of man's nature is good and beautiful,' he wrote, 'and destined to be fully enjoyed.' Writing, lecturing and travelling, he became a local celebrity with eminent friends—Emerson, Thoreau,

Carlyle. The travelling was inveterate, a series of 'speculative visits to possible better places . . . from which he was apt to return under premature, under passionate nostalgic reaction'. Henry James Senior was a genial, tender-hearted, inconsistent man, indulgent to his five children and heavily dependent on his wife. He was once criticised for being one of those 'purely ideal reformers, men who will lounge at their ease upon damask sofas and dream of a harmonic and beautiful world to be created hereafter'. His son recognised the mother's dominant role in the family: 'She was our life, she was our house, she was the keystone of the arch.' And he inherited her strength of will and capacity for devotion, hidden under a quiet, gentle exterior.

The works of Henry James Senior are no longer read today, but he had a gift for words which passed on to three of his five children. William James, the eldest (1842–1910), studied painting and then medicine, settled down to an academic career in America, became a distinguished philosopher and psychologist, and wrote two books, *The Principles of Psychology* and *The Varieties of Religious Experience*, which have survived (the former without benefit of Freud) to become living classics in a later age. His writing expresses a vigorous intellect and a most engaging personality. Henry, the second son, is a major figure in both English and American literature. Alice, the only daughter, became a permanent invalid, but her journal, published posthumously, is both humorous and eloquent, and constituted, as Henry said, 'a new claim for the family renown'.

The young Henry soon perceived that if his family was a happy one, it was happy on the basis of an odd way of life. 'We were for considerable periods, during our earliest time, nothing less than hotel children.' The frequent travelling reduced their schooling to 'small vague spasms'. Their father made it a matter of principle that they should receive no formal religious education. 'Our young liberty in respect to church-going was absolute and we might range at will, through the great city, from one place of worship and one form of faith to another, or might on occasion ignore them all equally, which was what we mainly did.' In his autobiography Henry sums up the intellectual consequence of this absence of a régime: 'The literal played in our education as small a part as it perhaps ever played in any, and we wholesomely breathed inconsistency and ate and drank contradictions . . . Method certainly never quite raged among us.'

It must have been a bewildering childhood. New York was above all a world of business, and 'whatever wasn't business, or exactly an office or a "store", places in which people sat close and made money, was just simply pleasure, sought, and sought only, in places in which people got tipsy'. In the James family no one 'sat close and made money': 'we were never in a single case, I think, for two generations, guilty of a stroke of business.' Inherited wealth had made Henry James Senior a man of leisure in a country in which leisure, for the male sex, was somehow not respectable. So at least his son had come to feel during his attempt to settle down in Cambridge, Massachusetts, in his late twenties: 'The young man who has not, in a word, an office in the business quarter of the town, with his name painted on the door, has but a limited place in the social system, finds no particular bough to perch upon.' Whether he *was* idle or not, he felt that he appeared so; and perhaps in Europe 'my vulgar idleness . . . would have been elegant leisure'. By now he aspired to be a man of letters, and felt himself subject to disapproval from two directions: in the eyes of the American world at large this was too irregular an occupation to be respectable, while in those of his father it was too specific not to be narrowing. A passage in the autobiography indicates the strange ground of paternal disapproval:

> What we were to do . . . was just to *be* something, something unconnected with specific doing, something free and uncommitted, something finer in short than being *that*, whatever it was, might consist of. The 'career of art' has again and again been deprecated and denounced, on the lips of anxiety or authority, as a departure from the world of business, of industry and respectability, the so-called regular life, but it was perhaps never elsewhere to know dissuasion on the very ground of its failing to uplift the spirit in the ways it most pretends to.

NOTES OF A SON AND BROTHER, Ch. 3

To distinguish thus between *being* and *doing*, and set the former above the latter, is the ideal and prerogative of aristocrats—and that is indeed what the James family were, in their way. It is also what Henry James's characters were to be. If he did not realise his father's ideal in his own life, in those of his characters he paid it an eloquent tribute.

There was a positive side to the family's detachment from social systems and institutions. The father's liberal-mindedness made for confidence and ease with his children. It enabled his daughter, for example, during her later nervous illness, to talk to him frankly of the possibility of suicide. He said that he did not consider it sinful, as an escape from suffering. The children grew up to inherit the intellectual and cultural freedom of the civilised world, and if the young Henry suffered from the sense of being 'outside' while others are 'inside', the sense of exclusion from the security of small communities, and found himself as a child much committed to 'gaping' at the lives of others and wishing he could be as they were, it was perhaps in this very habit of 'gaping' that he discovered his vocation to be a writer who creates by imagination other lives than his own. He had the critical intelligence to turn what might have been a disability into an asset, and became the critic *par excellence* of 'the mixture of manners' in modern Europe which has resulted largely from factors that conditioned his own upbringing: increasing affluence, easier travel, and the relaxation of old principles and constraints.

From his earliest years he was dominated by his brother William. It seemed 'as if he had gained such an advance of me in his sixteen months' experience of the world before mine began that I never for all the time of childhood and youth in the least caught up with him'. Henry seems to have felt second best to William most of his life. William was freely critical of his younger brother: he repeatedly referred to him as 'helpless', and in criticising his work would mix praise and blame in the most disconcerting manner. Henry accepted it meekly. Leon Edel, his biographer, has revealed the uncanny regularity with which until late in life Henry would suffer some sort of physical affliction whenever he and William were together for long, and how it would promptly cease when William went away. It is reasonable to suppose that this was another, unconscious reason for Henry to settle for Europe: he was no less ambitious than his brother, and he could not develop his ambition in his brother's shadow.

Abroad in Europe, the family was much turned in upon itself. Back in America, there were numerous uncles and aunts and cousins. The cousins evidently enjoyed some of the freedom and ease of Henry's own family. They seemed to him, in retrospect, to have lived 'by pure serenity, sociability and loquacity', whereas other children, 'trained and admonished, disciplined and governessed' seemed 'but *feebly* sophisticated'. Among these cousins one girl came to occupy the chief place in Henry's eyes. She was Mary ('Minnie') Temple, by all accounts a brilliantly attractive and intelligent girl. She developed tuberculosis and died at the age of twenty-four. Henry was one of a group of gifted young men, including his brother William, over whom she exercised a special fascination. Some of the most moving pages of his autobiography (the last chapter of *Notes of a Son and Brother*) are devoted to her memory. It has become a commonplace to say that she was the model for some of James's American heroines— Isabel Archer in *The Portrait of a Lady*, Mildred Theory in the story 'Georgina's Reasons', above all Milly Theale in *The Wings of the Dove*—and it is a strange experience, for anyone who has read those works, to turn to the autobiography and find the elderly James evoking in all the elaboration of his late style, and quoting in all the fresh simplicity of her own youthful one, a girl who does sound like a worthy model for these rare creatures:

> She was really to remain, for our appreciation, the supreme case of a taste for life as life, as personal living; of an endlessly active and yet somehow a careless, an illusionless, a sublimely forewarned curiosity about it: something that made her ... the very muse or amateur priestess of rash speculation. To express her in the mere terms of her restless young mind, one felt from the first, was to place her, by a perversion of the truth, under the shadow of female 'earnestness'— for which she was much too unliteral and too ironic; so that, superlatively personal and yet as independent, as 'off' into higher spaces,

> at a touch, as all the breadth of her sympathy and her courage could
> send her, she made it impossible to say whether she was just the
> most moving of maidens or a disengaged and dancing flame of
> thought. NOTES OF A SON AND BROTHER, Ch. 4

There could not be a better summary of what James intended and
achieved in some of his heroines.

If he kept a certain distance from her while she lived, it may
have been partly from a sense that some of her other admirers had
recently cut a more dashing figure than he had. The American
Civil War broke out in 1861, and though the two younger
brothers volunteered and fought on the Northern side, the
father discouraged both William and Henry from doing so. Any
question of enlisting was probably settled for Henry by his
suffering an obscure, undiagnosed injury to his back while
helping to put out a fire in a stable. It was to trouble him
intermittently for years: 'Some of my doses of pain were very
heavy; very weary were some of my months and years.' However, this accident may not have diminished his embarrassment
at being one of those who stayed at home. When Minnie died, in
1870, it seemed 'the end of our youth'. Henry James never
married. He was certainly attractive to women and enjoyed
their company, and his letters show how assiduously and grace-
fully he could cultivate their friendship, but as far as we know he
was never in love again.

James's childhood home had been in New York, but when
their European wanderings came to an end in 1860, his parents
settled in New England—first in Newport, then Boston, and
finally in Cambridge (Mass.), a suburb of Boston and the seat of
Harvard University. Boston was the capital of New England,
home of the 'New England conscience', a special offshoot of the
American Puritan tradition. The city, with its adjacent university
in half-rural surroundings, was more cultured and intellectual
than New York, but also more provincial, with a touch of com-
placency in its idealism. His novels *The Europeans* and *The
Bostonians* give contrasting pictures of the New England scene
(see Chapters 2 and 5).

Henry lived mostly at home for the next nine years. He

started to read Law at Harvard, gave it up, and set himself to write. In 1864, aged twenty-one, he published his first short story, anonymously, and his first book review. From the start there was a demand for his work from American journals. By the time he left for Europe again in 1869 he had published twelve stories and rejected the offer of a post as editor of the *North American Review*. He seems already to have felt sure of his vocation and of his need, as a creative writer, to guard his independence. Throughout his life he successfully resisted professional entanglement; a large measure of solitude was necessary for what he was going to accomplish. His reviews were mostly of novels: criticism and creation went hand in hand. He was reading the great English and French novelists and using their work as a standard by which to judge current American fiction. Occasionally he had the chance to review the latest work of one of the great Europeans: *Our Mutual Friend* in 1865, *Middlemarch* in 1873. His short stories were set in the America he knew. Obscurely, and no doubt unconsciously, they reflect early domestic tensions. His criticism, at this time, was better than his fiction.

Meanwhile he was discovering what a 'complex fate' it was to be an American; 'and one of the responsibilities it entails is fighting against a superstitious valuation of Europe'. His letters show that he sometimes felt lonely and that New England society could seem dull. But he was still some way from the conviction that his destiny lay in the Old World. A passage from a letter he wrote in 1867 gives a striking view of the opportunities he saw for himself as an American writer:

> We are Americans born—*il faut en prendre son parti*. I look upon it as a great blessing . . . We have exquisite qualities as a race, and it seems to me that we are ahead of the European races in the fact that more than either of them we can deal freely with forms of civilization not our own, can pick and choose and assimilate and in short (aesthetically &c) claim our property wherever we find it . . . We must of course have something of our own—something distinctive and homogeneous—and I take it that we shall find it in our moral consciousness, our unprecedented spiritual lightness and vigour.
>
> SELECTED LETTERS, ed. Edel, pp. 51–2

16

This passage is luminous in the light of James's later achievement. It begins to chart the possible cosmopolitan path that lay before him: he was indeed to 'deal freely' with the forms of European civilisation, and to bring to his analysis a distinctively American 'moral consciousness' that had its roots in the Puritanism of the early settlers; and the idea of 'picking and choosing and assimilating' points to the way he would use European manners as a quarry out of which to build an ideal moral world.

Early in 1869 he left for Europe. Italy, seen for the first time, was a revelation. In Venice, Florence and Rome the glory of Europe's past, perpetuated in stone, marble and canvas, was more splendidly before him than in any Northern city. 'The glory meant ever so many things at once, not only beauty and art and supreme design, but history and fame and power, the world in fine raised to the richest and noblest expression.' Those who have known and loved Florence and Rome only with their hideous modern accretions and disfigurements, and under the scourge of the motor car, would no doubt give their little fingers to have seen these cities as Henry James saw them a hundred years ago. The countryside was on the doorstep, and from Rome you could ride out into the Campagna, scattered with wild flowers and broken monuments and flocks of sheep, with sunburnt shepherds sleeping on the grass. Ill health sent him north again and limited funds determined his early return home; but it had been a decisive year. In the light of it, America now looked provincial and bare, and his aesthetic sense was starved. 'When I go to Europe again it will be, I think, from inanition of the eyes.'

He went again in 1872 and stayed for two years, mostly in Italy. He spent a very happy winter in Rome. There was a sizeable colony of hospitable American expatriates and it was with them, not with Italians, that he spent his time. Many of them were artists and all the artists, he soon saw, were failures. It must have been a warning, if he needed one. It also gave him the material for his second novel, *Roderick Hudson*. Italy was beautiful, but he recognised that, 'lovely and desirable though it was', it 'didn't seem as a permanent residence to lead to anything'.

'You feel altogether out of the current of modern civilisation.' Italian society remained closed to him, and though it was a country where foreigners could easily feel at home, an American colony offered him limited material as a novelist. But visually, Italy made an important contribution to the ideal world his artist's imagination was building out of the materials of Europe.

American magazines were ready to publish his impressions of Europe. In them he begins to rationalise his preference for the Old World. Of English life he wrote: 'The tone of things is, somehow, heavier than with us; manners and modes are more absolute and positive; they seem to swarm and thicken the air about you. Morally and physically it is a denser air than ours. We seem loosely hung together at home, compared with the English, every man of whom is a tight fit in his place.' Later, in his book on Hawthorne (1879), he related this superior 'density' of Europe to the needs of a novelist: 'It is on manners, customs, usages, habits, forms, upon all these things matured and established, that a novelist lives—they are the very stuff that his work is made of.' He wanted both life and art to have 'form'—and American life had less than he needed. 'To produce some little exemplary works of art is my narrow and lowly dream. They are to have less "brain" than *Middlemarch*; but (I boldly proclaim it) they are to have more *form*.'

He had been writing for ten years but had not yet published a volume. However, the demand for his work gradually increased, and he was beginning to keep himself by his pen. He seems to have decided early in his career that he could not be popular, but though he might give up the ambition of ever being 'a free-going and light-paced enough writer to please the multitude', this did not mean he should not aspire to public recognition and a certain worldly success. He planned his career with energy and a good business sense, and managed its practical and financial side until 1899, when he put it in the hands of a literary agent.

In 1875 *Roderick Hudson* was serialised and he published a volume of stories, *A Passionate Pilgrim*, and one of essays, *Transatlantic Sketches*. All were well received by American critics, but after a strenuous stint of reviewing in New York, he left in the autumn for Paris and spent a year there, supported partly by a contract to supply a regular 'Paris Letter' for the *New York Tribune*. It was now the turn of France to enthral him.

He was already a competent speaker and writer of the language. He had been reading French novelists and critics for years, and invoking their standards of realism and technical competence in his reviews of American fiction. Balzac (1799–1850), whom he discovered in his late teens, impressed and influenced him most of all. Superficially, with its immense accumulations of background detail, its obvious psychological and moral crudities, its rash generalisations, Balzac's work may seem to have little in common with James's, but James expressed his lasting fascination in a series of essays on the French novelist dating from 1878 to 1905. He called Balzac 'the father of us all', saw him as the first truly professional novelist, seriously devoted to his art, and admired the scale and architecture of his achievement: not just a string of stories, but *La Comédie Humaine*, a single complex fictive structure. When he revised his fiction, in his sixties, for the New York Edition, James carefully planned for twenty-three volumes, the same number as in the current edition of *La Comédie Humaine*. There might have been great English novelists—James was by now deeply impressed by the work of George Eliot—but the English were aesthetically naïve. Balzac had given the art of fiction its proper dignity.

Flaubert, Zola, Maupassant, Daudet, Edmond de Goncourt—James met all these writers in Paris and found himself casually welcome at their long Sunday afternoon discussions in Flaubert's house. Here, if anywhere, was the 'serious male interest' he had missed in America and Italy. The talk was extraordinarily free by English or American standards: James had jumped across a cultural gap and morally speaking he was breathing a lighter air. '*Tu vois que je suis dans les conseils des dieux—je suis lancé en plein Olympe.*' He learned from them a new view of the relation between art and morality. They had consciously emancipated themselves from the moral values of their society. The serious French writer had never been able to see in the French bourgeoisie an embodiment of moral values which he could sincerely endorse—there had been, and could have been, no French Jane Austen. Later English novelists were more critical of middle-class values, but that was a different matter from the complete rejection of bourgeois values in the work of Balzac, Stendhal and Flaubert.

The writers James met in Paris in the 1870s, twenty years after the publication of *Madame Bovary* and *Les Fleurs du Mal*, took it for granted that the writer's responsibility was to the aesthetic requirements of his art rather than to the moral prejudices of his public. There was no question of teaching their readers a moral lesson. The emphasis therefore fell on form rather than sub-stance—or rather, as James put it, 'Form alone takes and holds and preserves substance.' Everything must be *shown*. The more a writer merely referred to things, instead of representing them, the less he was an artist. And the particular was preferred to the general. In his own work James concentrated increasingly on the particular—this is one reason why his later works are harder to read, the particularity taking the form of increasingly fine moral discrimination, rather than increasingly detailed physical speci-fication—and though in this he evidently followed the require-ments of his own imagination, the French tradition must have confirmed and encouraged his interest in technique and method.

At the same time he had reservations about the French. They were very emancipated but strangely narrow. This was partly the habitual French exclusiveness, that assumption of their cultural superiority over other nations which can make them so curiously provincial in outlook; but there was also the impression that these writers of the second half of the century were dealing with life at a lower level and in a meaner spirit than their great predecessors. Flaubert dwarfed the others, yet the author of *Madame Bovary*, an undoubted masterpiece, was, for James, an example of mag-nificent devotion to his art but also of a curious spiritual failure. The English novelists, on the other hand, were morally timid, less exploratory, technically and aesthetically naïve; but who among the French could match Dickens's exuberance, or the spiritual fineness of George Eliot? He read the latter's *Daniel*

Deronda (1876) in Paris and felt 'the superiority of English culture and the English mind to the French'. '*Ces messieurs*', he wrote later of Zola and the 'naturalists', 'seem to me to have lost the perception of anything in nature except the genital organs.' James's ethical sensibility was conditioned by his Protestant upbringing to treat moral problems as determinant in human conduct, whereas the French tended to stress the determining power of physical and social conditions.

In Paris he also met the Russian novelist Turgenev (1818–83). James had already admired his work, and was soon delighted with the man. The two spent a good deal of time together. Some of what James learned from Turgenev is recorded in his preface to *The Portrait of a Lady*, where he recalls Turgenev telling him how he usually began composition with a single character, a stray disposable figure, and then looked for 'the right relations . . . the complications they would be most likely to produce and to feel'—not that this was always James's method: the Notebooks show us how often he began with a situation, and after gradual elaboration and refinement, arrived at characters possibly very different from those suggested by the original anecdote. James also admired the poetic aura surrounding Turgenev's heroines and what he called their 'moral beauty'. Both writers were profound psychologists and conscious stylists, and neither was particularly interested in general ideas. More by nationality than by temperament, Turgenev had to concern himself with questions of social reform and revolution. His sympathies were liberal, but his finely discriminating, slightly ironical vision is much more akin to James's than to his great Russian contemporaries Tolstoy and Dostoievsky. In *The Princess Casamassima*, his one major novel which deals with the possibility of social upheaval, James shows qualities which recall Turgenev: sympathy combined with scrupulous detachment, an appreciation of the old world together with an understanding of those who wish to destroy it, and a perception of the complex variety of personal motives in those who join in a common cause.

After a year in France, during which he wrote his third novel,

The American, James moved to London in 1876 and took rooms in Bolton Street, off Piccadilly. Looking back on this decisive move, he wrote in his Notebook five years later:

> I came to London as a complete stranger, and today I know much too many people. *J'y suis absolument comme chez moi* . . . It is difficult to speak adequately or justly of London . . . You can draw up a tremendous list of reasons why it should be insupportable. The fogs, the smoke, the dirt, the darkness, the wet, the distances, the ugliness, the brutal size of the place, the horrible numerosity of society, the manner in which this senseless bigness is fatal to amenity, to convenience, to conversation, to good manners—all this and much more you may expatiate upon. You may call it dreary, heavy, stupid, dull, inhuman, vulgar at heart and tiresome in form . . . But these are occasional moods, and for one who takes it as I take it, London is on the whole the most possible form of life. I take it as an artist and as a bachelor; as one who has the passion of observation and whose business is the study of human life. It is the biggest aggregation of human life—the most complete compendium of the world . . . I felt all this in that autumn of 1876 . . . I had very few friends, the season was of the darkest and wettest; but I was in a state of deep delight. I had complete liberty, and the prospect of profitable work. I used to take long walks in the rain. I took possession of London; I felt it to be the right place.

NOTEBOOKS, pp. 27–8

England became his home for the rest of his life. He found the English friendly and hospitable and soon got a footing in London society. After a day's writing, he would dine out—during the winter of 1878–9 he is said to have accepted 140 invitations—and then take a long roundabout walk home through the grimy streets and read 'the hard prose of misery' among London's poor. He was introduced to various London clubs, where he observed the figures of the famous at their ease, and was invited to English country houses. There he enjoyed 'that rural hospitality which is the great invention of the English people and the most perfect expression of their character'; but he also remarked on 'that great total of labour and poverty on whose enormous base all the luxury and leisure of English country houses are built up'. He was laying in material 'at the rate of a ton a day'. He admired the English, called them 'the strongest and richest race in the world', and aspired to be their 'moral portrait-painter'.

There was also much to criticise. The English were dull and philistine. They somehow had style without having a sense of style, and there seemed to be a mysterious connection between their happy ease of manner and the intellectual void—or as James more gently put it, 'the deep intellectual repose'—that lay behind it.

The later tales abound in sharp references to English inanity. As a writer, he found the English a rich subject but an indifferent, because a largely uncritical, audience. 'They have not a spontaneous artistic life . . . It is impossible to live much among them, to be a spectator of their habits, their manners, their arrangements, without perceiving that the artistic point of view is the last that they naturally take.'

A passage from the third, unfinished part of his autobiography, *The Middle Years,* records the sort of relish he took in the outward aspects of the London scene. It concerns an eating-house called 'The Albany', consisting of 'small compartments, narrow as horse-stalls, formed by the hard straight backs of hard wooden benches and accommodating respectively two pairs of feeders, who were thus so closely face to face as fairly to threaten with knife and fork each other's more forward features'. He goes on to connect the details of the scene with the general ground of his delight in European as opposed to American civilisation. In its way, it's as good an explanation as anything he wrote, of what he wanted and found in Europe:

> The scene was sordid, the arrangements primitive, the detail of the procedure, as it struck me, wellnigh of the rudest; yet I remember rejoicing in it all—as one indeed might perfectly rejoice in the juiciness of joints and the abundance of accessory pudding; for I said to myself under every shock and at the hint of every savour that this was what it was for an exhibition to reek of local colour, and one could dispense with a napkin, with a crusty roll, with room for one's elbows or one's feet, with an immunity from intermittence of the 'plain boiled', much better than one could dispense with that.

There were restaurants galore even at that time in New York and in Boston, but I had never before had to do with an eating-house and had not yet seen the little old English world of Dickens, let alone of the ever-haunting Hogarth, of Smollett and of Boswell, drenched with such a flood of light . . . Every face was a documentary scrap, half a dozen broken words to piece with half a dozen others, and so on and on; every sound was strong, whether rich and fine or only queer and coarse; everything in this order drew a positive sweetness from never being—whatever else it was—gracelessly flat. The very rudeness was ripe, the very commonness conscious—that is, not related to mere other forms of the same, but to matters as different as possible, into which it shaded off and off or up and up; the image in fine was organic, rounded and complete, as definite as a Dutch picture of low life hung on a museum wall.

THE MIDDLE YEARS, Ch. 4

After a few years he felt the need to resist the pressures of London's social life and be more selective in his acquaintance. He would arrange to be abroad during the London 'season' and at home in late summer when the fashionable people were in the country. He consorted more with fellow-writers and artists. Those he met over the years include Tennyson, George Eliot, Ruskin, Browning, Meredith, Matthew Arnold, Trollope, Leslie Stephen, George du Maurier, Robert Louis Stevenson, Sargent, Kipling, Edmund Gosse, Shaw, Wells, Conrad, Ford Madox Ford, G. K. Chesterton, Max Beerbohm, Rupert Brooke, and Virginia Woolf.

All the time he was writing hard. America was not forgotten: three of his next five novels—*The Europeans*, *Washington Square* and *The Bostonians*—are set wholly in the New World, and during the next ten years he wrote most of his 'international' fiction. It was only from the middle 1880s that he found his subjects mostly within the English social scene. In 1883 Macmillans brought out a pocket edition of his fiction in fourteen volumes; but that was nothing to rest on: 'I shall be forty years old in April next: it's a horrible fact . . . I must make some great efforts during the next few years, if I wish not to have been on the whole a failure. I shall have been a failure unless I do something *great*.' Ironically, when he wrote these words he had passed the period of his greatest popular success; this had attended 'Daisy Miller' (1878) and the other brilliant international tales of that time, and the early novels up to and including *The Portrait of a Lady* (1881). In spite of a few discerning critics, his novels from now on were indifferently received on both sides of the Atlantic. His reputation had overtaken his income, and though the former was never quite eclipsed, the latter was only kept at a respectable level by his very prolific output. James had some hard things to say about his public and its failure to appreciate what he was doing, on any but 'infantile grounds'. Yet publishers continued to issue his novels and tales not only in book form but in magazines, and the difficulty of his later works makes this a tribute to the literary standards of the day.

He followed the glaring failure of his two great novels *The Bostonians* and *The Princess Casamassima*, both published in 1886, with a group of *nouvelles* or long short stories that are among his very best: 'The Aspern Papers', 'A London Life', 'The Lesson of the Master', 'The Patagonia' and 'The Pupil'. At the same time he was writing another major novel, *The Tragic Muse* (1890), which in subject-matter looks forward to the next phase of his career, his disastrous affair with the theatre.

He had been an enthusiastic theatre-goer in Paris and London, and had long ago thought of writing for the stage. Now, with his fiction selling poorly in book form, he found himself short of money. Edward Compton, a young English actor with his own troupe, asked James if he wouldn't adapt his novel *The American* for the stage. He did so, changing the ending to a happy one. The play had a moderately successful run, but yielded a negligible revenue. He then wrote four plays that didn't even get into production. *Guy Domville* eventually reached the London stage in 1895. The play was applauded from the expensive seats and booed from the cheap ones. When James took a curtain call he was hooted. Although it ran for a month, and was given favourable notices by Shaw, Wells and Arnold Bennett, the play's relative failure was a crushing blow for James. In failing to write successfully for the stage, he joined an illustrious company of 19th-century poets and novelists. His dialogue was too 'literary'. His curiously inconsistent attitude to the theatre is reflected in 'Nona Vincent', a tale of 1892, where he projects it upon the hero. He had evidently failed to take the measure of this enterprise.

James was past fifty. In the twelve years since he had buoyantly reformulated his ambition to 'do something *great*', three major novels had been greeted with indifference or hostility and now his theatrical venture had collapsed in tepid applause. It may well have looked like the end of his career. He spoke of a 'black abyss', and there seems to be no doubt that he was profoundly dismayed and discouraged. Somehow he made an almost immediate recovery and turned back to the writing of fiction. From the experience of writing plays he evolved—or at least convinced himself that he was evolving—a new principle for the composition of a novel: that of the 'scenario'. This is explained in the preface to *The Awkward Age* (1899), where he describes how he composed that novel like 'the successive Acts of a Play'. This means that it has the special *objectivity* of drama, which derives from the playwright's inability to 'go behind' his characters in the way a novelist can. The idea was 'to make the presented occasion tell all its story itself, remain shut up in its own presence and yet on that patch of staked-out ground become thoroughly interesting and remain thoroughly clear'. Dialogue therefore predominates over narrative, which restricts itself to noting what is outwardly visible, such as could be seen or heard on the stage, or what an intelligent observer might have inferred. *The Awkward Age* is a highly original and, on its own terms, successful novel, but it may be doubted whether the principle of the scenario was quite such a discovery as James felt at the time. In his earlier fiction, especially in some of the tales, he had been tending in that direction. Now he rationalised the tendency and developed it further.

The next decade was as prolific as any in his career: he wrote eight novels and some thirty tales. He found new subjects—in particular the predicament of the child growing up into a corrupt and largely indifferent adult world—and reworked old themes in new ways. His style became more subtle and elaborate, combining a highly idiosyncratic syntax with a more colloquial idiom and a greater richness of metaphor, and he used it to cover a wide range of experience and variety of effects: brilliant comic dialogue in *What Maisie Knew* and *The Awkward Age*; racy satirical narration in 'The Death of the Lion', 'The Birthplace' and 'The Papers'; tragic intensity in *The Wings of the Dove* and 'The Beast in the Jungle'; mystery and terror in 'The Turn of the Screw' and 'The Jolly Corner'.

The style of his own life changed too. Since 1876 he had been based in London, first in lodgings off Piccadilly, then in a more spacious flat in Kensington. Every year he had travelled on the continent, sometimes staying several months in Italy, and had twice returned to America. He had been used to getting on with his writing wherever he happened to be—in hotels and lodgings and other people's houses. Now he engaged the services of a typist, and the size of the early typewriters made composition a less movable activity. At the same time he began to think of having a house of his own in the country, in England. He successfully increased his income with literary commissions and in 1897 was able to lease, and later to buy, Lamb House, a large, dignified 18th-century house in the small town of Rye on the Sussex coast. He bought old furniture and settled in with evident delight: 'After so many years of London flats and other fearsome fragilities, I feel quite housed in a feudal fortress.' His staff comprised the drunken couple who had run his London flat, a housemaid, a 'house-boy', a part-time gardener, and the typist. He learned to bicycle and took long rides and walks in the country. He took a benevolent interest in local society, enjoyed having friends and relations to stay, and kept in touch with London life by means of copious telegrams, a practice commemorated in the fine tale of 1898, 'In the Cage'.

The elderly James is richly commemorated in the anecdotes of his contemporaries, some of which have been delightfully collected by Simon Nowell-Smith in *The Legend of the Master*. By now he was quite a famous figure, respected by his contemporaries in the world of letters and venerated by some of his juniors—in particular by a number of bright young men including the writers Hugh Walpole, Desmond McCarthy and Compton Mackenzie. This did not mean that his books sold any better than before, or that criticism was more discerning— merely that reviewers approached them with more respect than in his middle period. But he no longer expected to be appreciated as a writer. In 1915 H. G. Wells, whom James had befriended and encouraged, published a clever but malicious attack on his work in a book called *Boon*:

> The elaborate, copious emptiness of the whole Henry James exploit is only redeemed and made endurable by the elaborate, copious wit . . . Having first made sure that he has scarcely anything left to express, he then sets to work to express it, with an industry, a wealth of intellectual stuff that dwarfs Newton . . . He brings up every device of language to state and define. Bare verbs he rarely tolerates. He splits his infinitives and fills them up with adverbial stuffing. He presses the passing colloquialism into his service. His vast paragraphs sweat and struggle . . . It is leviathan retrieving a pebble. It is a magnificent but painful hippopotamus resolved at any cost, even at the cost of its dignity, upon picking up a pea which has got into a corner of its den. Most things, it insists, are beyond it, but it can, at any rate, modestly, and with an artistic singleness of mind, pick up that pea . . .

James answered this attack with extraordinary gentleness and civility.

After the great series of novels written between 1896 and 1904, which some regard as the summit of his achievement— *The Spoils of Poynton*, *What Maisie Knew*, *The Awkward Age*, *The Ambassadors*, *The Wings of the Dove* and *The Golden Bowl*— James set sail for America. He had not been back for twenty years and was curious. He would see William and his family, and other friends. He would also visit the South and West, which were new to him. There was a question of a collected American edition of his works. He lectured to enthusiastic audiences on 'The Lesson of Balzac', making a plea for a more discerning criticism of fiction. It was a successful trip, lasting nearly a year, and he recorded his impressions in *The American Scene*, which has been called 'one of the very best books about modern America'.

James was struck by the absence of local character, civic pride, and social structure and standards. He found a 'monotony of acquiescence'. New developments were 'expensively provisional' and the land was being raped by commercial exploitation. Whether he knew it or not, he was writing a diagnosis of the general polluting tendency of modern Western life. What he saw happening in America has subsequently spoiled Europe. The tone of the writing is both heavily portentous and full of humour. He notices, for example, the way Americans are always eating 'candy', and wonders, if 'so much purchasing-power can flow to the supposedly superfluous',

> what such facts represented, what light they might throw upon manners and wages. Wages, in the country at large, *are* largely manners—the only manners, I think it fair to say, one mostly encounters; the market and the home therefore look alike dazzling, at first, in this reflected, many-coloured lustre. It speaks somehow, beyond anything else, of the diffused sense of material ease—since the solicitation of sugar couldn't be so hugely and artfully organised if the response were not clearly proportionate . . . The wage-earners, the toilers of old, notably in other climes, were known by the wealth of their songs; and has it, on these lines, been given to the American people to be known by the number of their 'candies'?   Ch. 5

In 1905 he began to revise his fiction for a collected edition, published by Scribners and known as the New York Edition. This included many of the tales and all his best novels, with the notable exceptions of *The Europeans*, *Washington Square* and *The Bostonians*, all set in America. In the case of *The Bostonians*, at least, this omission was on the publisher's insistence and not because James no longer thought well of it. To each volume he wrote a long preface, and these documents throw much light on the problems of composition as James saw them. The reader will find many quotations from them in this study. He also revised in detail the texts of everything he included. His alterations were most numerous in the early works, especially *Roderick Hudson* and *The American*, and the experienced reader can often smell them out. It is doubtful whether they always constitute an improvement. Unrevised texts of the novels are regrettably out of print and hard to come by, but the great current edition of the tales by Leon Edel gives them all in their unrevised form. The poor sales of the New York Edition were a severe disappointment to James.

His other big enterprise of these years was the autobiography, begun in 1911 after his brother William's death. He meant it partly as a tribute to his family, especially his father and William, as the title of the second volume, *Notes of a Son and Brother*, shows. The unfinished third volume, *The Middle Years*, carries the reader up to the time of his settlement in London in the 1870s.

In 1914 he began another major novel, *The Ivory Tower*, but with the outbreak of war he found he could not go on with it. The war horrified him:

> How can what is going on not be to one as a huge horror of blackness? ... The plunge of civilisation into this abyss of blood and darkness by the wanton feat of those two infamous autocrats is a thing that so gives away the whole long age during which we have supposed the world to be, with whatever abatement, gradually bettering, that to have to take it all now for what the treacherous years were all the while really making for and *meaning* is too tragic for any words. Letter to Howard Sturgis

He threw himself energetically into practical work, helping Belgian refugees, visiting the wounded in hospital and entertaining them at his London flat. The German threat made him realise how much of an Englishman he had become and he applied for naturalisation, which was immediately granted under the auspices of Asquith, the Prime Minister, a personal friend.

James continued into his seventies to show an extraordinary physical and mental appetite for life, visiting and entertaining profusely, and habitually taking long walks of three hours or more in the afternoons. Then in December 1915 he suffered a stroke and was an invalid until his death three months later. On New Year's Day 1916 he was awarded the Order of Merit. He was the third novelist, after Meredith and Hardy, to be thus honoured.

James did not, like Proust, withdraw from life to get on with his work; the huge volume of his correspondence, still uncollected, testifies to his loving and painstaking involvement in the lives of others. Yet behind this there was 'the essential loneliness of my life . . . This loneliness . . . what is it still but the deepest thing about one?' This was the condition of so much creation. Desmond McCarthy has recorded the following conversation with 'the Master':

> It occurred after a luncheon party of which he had been, as they say, 'the life'. We happened to be drinking our coffee together while the rest of the party had moved on to the verandah. 'What a charming picture they make,' he said, with his great head aslant, 'the women there with their embroidery, the . . .' There was nothing in his words, anybody might have spoken them; but in his attitude, in his voice, in his whole being at that moment, I divined such complete detachment, that I was startled into speaking out of myself: 'I can't bear to look at life like that,' I blurted out, 'I want to be in everything. Perhaps that is why I cannot *write*, it makes me feel absolutely alone . . .' The effect of this confession upon him was instantaneous and surprising. He leant forward and grasped my arm excitedly: 'Yes, it is solitude. If it runs after you and catches you, well and good. But for heaven's sake don't run after *it*. It is absolute solitude.' And he got up hurriedly and joined the others.

It seems that, like Stendhal, James's sensibility was somehow out of tune with—one might say, in advance of—his time. Stendhal predicted, more or less correctly, that it would take a hundred years for his work to come into its own. James has not had to wait as long as that: over the last forty years he has received a great deal of critical attention and acclaim, and many cheap editions of his works have testified to his modern popularity.

2

The Europeans (1878)

This was James's fourth novel. Shorter than its predecessors and more completely successful, it is a pastoral and romantic comedy of great charm, dealing lightly but not superficially with questions of manners and morals and the good life. It tells the story of a highly respectable New England family visited by two cousins who, though American in origin, have lived all their lives in Europe. The novel thus presents the 'international situation' so common in James, but an unusual version of it: usually the Americans come to Europe; only in a few stories and in no other novel is the traffic the other way.

The Europeans are Felix Young, a high-spirited, artistic youth, and his very different married elder sister Eugenia, Baroness Münster. They arrive in Boston on a cold day in spring, 'upwards of thirty years since', to visit their American cousins the Wentworths. They come with high hopes and high standards, and the New England society that welcomes them is in its way a highly civilised one. This is not the America of the pioneers or the Wild West, nor is it at all obviously the America that James himself described with tongue in cheek in his critical study of the American novelist Nathaniel Hawthorne, written a year after *The Europeans:*

> One might enumerate the items of high civilisation, as it exists in other countries, which are absent from the texture of American life, until it should become a wonder to know what is left. No State, in the European sense of the word, and indeed barely a specific national name. No sovereign, no court, no personal loyalty, no aristocracy, no church, no clergy, no army, no diplomatic service, no country gentlemen, no palaces, no castles, nor manors,

nor old country houses, nor parsonages, nor thatched cottages, nor ivied ruins; no cathedrals, nor abbeys, nor little Norman churches; no great Universities, nor public schools—no Oxford, nor Eton, nor Harrow; no literature, no novels, no museums, no pictures, no political society, no sporting class—no Epsom nor Ascot! Some such list as that might be drawn up of the absent things in American life—especially in the American life of forty years ago, the effect of which, upon an English or a French imagination, would probably as a general thing be appalling.

Many of these items are of course absent from the scene that unfolds, but what's there is far from giving an impression of a lack of social forms. The Wentworths live in an ordered, peopled countryside a few miles from the city of Boston and the University of Harvard. James describes the Sunday morning scene with affectionate appreciation:

> The flowering shrubs and the neatly-disposed plants were basking in the abundant light and warmth; the transparent shade of the great elms—they were magnificent trees—seemed to thicken by the hour; and the intensely habitual stillness offered a submissive medium to the sound of a distant church-bell . . . It was an ancient house—ancient in the sense of being eighty years old; it was built of wood, painted a clean, clear, faded grey, and adorned along the front, at intervals, with flat wooden pilasters, painted white . . . And the front door of the big, unguarded home stood open, with the trustfulness of the golden age; or, what is more to the purpose, with that of New England's silvery prime . . . There was no library in the house, but there were books in all the rooms. None of them were forbidden books . . .   Ch. 2, p. 1

There may not be an aristocracy in New England, but as Mr. Wentworth retorts when reminded that his European cousin is the wife of a prince, 'We are all Princes here, and I don't know of any palace in this neighbourhood that is to let.' It is in fact one civilisation confronting two representatives of another, with a common language and ties of kinship making for the greatest possible facility of contact. The New England of this novel has a social coherence, a stability based on tradition, which distinguish it from the urban society of *The Bostonians*, written eight years

33

later and not, like *The Europeans*, set back in time. This setting back may perhaps have been a way of isolating and framing certain elements of American society that James had known in his youth and that seemed to him best fitted to compose into a somewhat idealised picture of an American way of life, coherent enough to offer a clear contrast and alternative to European values, and small enough for a short novel. Certainly, as *The Bostonians* shows with its more satirical pictures of Boston and New York, this was not the only America that James knew, but it is perhaps the most endearing portrait of American life to be found in his work—and this in part because of its very provinciality.

In his preface to Volume XI of the New York Edition ('Lady Barberina'), which includes several of his international stories, James mentions the 'old rigours of separation' that in the past have kept societies apart and distinct, and the symptoms among modern educated people of 'a common intelligence and a social fusion tending to abridge them'; and he goes on to speak of 'the many-coloured sanctity of such rigours in general, which have hitherto made countries smaller but kept the globe larger, and by which immediate strangeness, immediate beauty, immediate curiosity were so much fostered'. This is very much what *The Europeans* is about. In the same preface he speaks of 'the pity and the misery and the greater or less grotesqueness of the courageous, or even of the timid, missing their lives beyond certain stiff barriers', and he looks forward to 'their more and more steadily making out their opportunities and their possible communications' as social life becomes less confined in the future. *The Europeans* is the story of two young people who do indeed succeed, without violence or misery, in 'making out their opportunities and their possible communications' in spite of 'certain stiff barriers'.

James's criticism of his little New England world, however muted by affection, centres quite explicitly on its over-earnest preoccupation with duty: with what one ought to be, or do, rather than with what one is. The consequence, we see, is that these people don't know how to be happy. They live well, both materially and morally, but without joy. The point is made in a passage which introduces the Wentworths' discussion of how they are to accommodate their European cousins:

> If you had been present, it would probably not have seemed to you that the advent of these brilliant strangers was treated as an exhilarating occurrence, a pleasure the more in this tranquil household, a prospective source of entertainment. This was not Mr. Wentworth's way of treating any human occurrence. The sudden irruption into the well-ordered consciousness of the Wentworths of an element not allowed for in its usual scheme of obligations, required a readjustment of that sense of responsibility which constituted its principal furniture. To consider an event, crudely and baldly, in the light of the pleasure it might bring them, was an intellectual exercise with which Felix Young's American cousins were almost wholly unacquainted, and which they scarcely supposed to be largely pursued in any section of human society. The arrival of Felix and his sister was a satisfaction, but it was a singularly joyless and inelastic satisfaction. It was an extenson of duty, of the exercise of the more recondite virtues.   Ch. 4, p. 44

This is the Protestant ethos, and a particular strain of it which the Puritans took with them to the New World in the 17th century and which survives to this day, when it can still be detected in well-brought-up young Americans from the East Coast. They see an opposition, almost an incompatibility, between pleasure and duty, where none necessarily exists. It is what philosophers call a false dichotomy; and a great deal of comedy arises out of the failure of their theory to fit the facts.

The dichotomy is diagnosed with great assurance by Felix Young, the young man whose 'brilliantly healthy nature' is a living refutation of it and proves at once so perplexing and so irresistible to his cousins:

> 'No, they are not gay,' Felix admitted. 'They are sober; they are even severe. They are of a pensive cast; they take things hard. I think there is something the matter with them; they have some melancholy memory or some depressing expectation. It's not the epicurean temperament. My uncle, Mr. Wentworth, is a tremendously high-toned old fellow; he looks as if he were undergoing

martyrdom, not by fire, but by freezing. But we shall cheer them up; we shall do them good. They will take a good deal of stirring up; but they are wonderfully kind and gentle. And they are appreciative. They think one clever; they think one remarkable.'

Ch. 3, p. 33

The most 'appreciative' of them all is his younger cousin Gertrude, 'a peculiar girl' who 'had to struggle with a great accumulation of obstructions, both of the subjective, as the metaphysicians say, and of the objective order; and indeed it is no small part of the purpose of this little history to set forth her struggle'. She is 'peculiar' only by the standards of her American background and because her nature is profoundly at odds with the ethos in which she has grown up. This is beautifully shown, long before it's diagnosed, on her first appearance:

'Gertrude [says her elder sister Charlotte], are you very sure you had better not go to church?'

Gertrude looked at her a moment, plucked a small sprig from a lilac-bush, smelled it and threw it away. 'I am not very sure of anything!' she answered.

The other young lady looked straight past her, at the distant pond, which lay shining between the long banks of fir trees. Then she said in a very soft voice, 'This is the key of the dining-room closet. I think you had better have it, if anyone should want anything.'

'Who is there to want anything?' Gertrude demanded. 'I shall be all alone in the house.'

'Someone may come', said her companion.

'Do you mean Mr. Brand?'

'Yes, Gertrude. He may like a piece of cake.'

'I don't like men that are always eating cake!' Gertrude declared, giving a pull at the lilac-bush.

Her companion glanced at her, and then looked down on the ground. 'I think father expected you would come to church,' she said. 'What shall I say to him?'

'Say I have a bad headache.'

'Would that be true?' asked the elder lady, looking straight at the pond again.

'No, Charlotte,' said the younger one simply.

Charlotte transferred her quiet eyes to her companion's face. 'I am afraid you are feeling restless.'

'I am feeling as I always feel,' Gertrude replied in the same tone.

Ch. 2, p. 19

The essential elements of the situation are all there: in Charlotte, moral anxiety side by side with concern for physical well-being ('He may like a piece of cake'); preoccupation with duty ('are you very sure you had better not go to church?') together with anxiety about the future ('I think you had better have it, if anyone should want anything'), and a scrupulous veracity—and against that, the other girl with her perverse answers, and the natural spring scene with the lilac-bush being pulled and 'the distant pond, which lay shining between the long banks of fir trees'.

Gertrude Wentworth is 'explained' by her cousin Felix, towards the end of the novel, by which time her response to the alternative he offers has been fully shown:

'She has always been a dormant nature. She was waiting for a touchstone. But now she is beginning to awaken ... She doesn't care for abstractions. Now I think the contrary is what you have always fancied—is the basis on which you have been building. She is extremely preoccupied with the concrete. I care for the concrete too. But Gertrude is stronger than I; she whirls me along!'

Ch. 10, p. 140

This is one half of the plot, brought to a happy conclusion when her sister and even her former lover are brought to urge Mr. Wentworth to consent, reluctantly, to her marriage to Felix.

The other half concerns the other European, Felix's elder sister Eugenia. She is morganatically married to the younger brother of a German princeling, who for political reasons wants to dissolve the marriage and has half succeeded in doing so. She sets her cap at Robert Acton, cousin of the Wentworths and a regular member of their little circle. Here it is the European who is shown to be inadequate, and unlike Gertrude she cannot rise to the occasion, so the mooted marriage comes to nothing. What's wrong with Eugenia is not difficult to feel, but less easy to

37

pin down. None of the other characters diagnoses it as explicitly as Felix diagnoses what afflicts the Americans, and James, perhaps consciously compensating for this, devotes more explanation to her than to the others. Robert Acton sums it up in a way when he says to himself 'She is not honest . . . she is a woman who will lie.' But this occurs late in the story, and if we haven't felt the trouble long before this we have missed the point. We can feel it already in the very first scene, in the hotel in Boston, where her over-indulged displeasure at the unfamiliar urban scene and the bad weather contrasts unfavourably with her brother's generous appreciation of everything new and strange.

When she arrives at the Wentworths, her manner can only be described as vulgar, in comparison with their reticence. This is her tone:

> 'Ah, there comes a moment in life when one reverts, irresistibly, to one's natural ties—to one's natural affections. You must have found that!' said Eugenia.
>
> Mr. Wentworth had been told the day before by Felix that Eugenia was very clever, very brilliant, and the information had held him in some suspense. This was the cleverness, he supposed; the brilliancy was beginning. 'Yes, the natural affections are very strong,' he murmured.
>
> 'In some people,' the Baroness declared. 'Not in all.' Charlotte was walking beside her; she took hold of her hand again, smiling always. 'And you, *cousine*, where did you get that enchanting complexion?' she went on; 'such lilies and roses!'   Ch. 3, p. 37

It's vulgar because it's patronising, and the patronising is felt in the tendency to generalise which doesn't respect the 'otherness' of other people. That the Americans largely fail to see through her, although they don't enjoy her tone, is a function of their provinciality for which we are not encouraged to blame them. Here she is again:

> Eugenia kissed her, as she had kissed the other young women, and then held her off a little, looking at her. 'Now this is quite another *type*', she said; she pronounced the word in the French manner. 'This is a different outline, my uncle, a different character, from that

of your own daughters. This, Felix,' she went on, 'is very much
more what we have always thought of as the American type.'

Ch. 3, p. 41

It's not just that she's outspoken—Felix is that too, but with him
it doesn't jar, unless when he is persuading Mr. Wentworth to
sit for his portrait:

> 'I should like to do your head, sir,' said Felix to his uncle one
> evening, before them all . . . 'I think I should make a very fine thing
> of it. It's an interesting head; it's very medieval.'
>
> Mr. Wentworth looked grave; he felt awkwardly, as if all the
> company had come in and found him standing before the looking-
> glass. 'The Lord made it,' he said. 'I don't think it is for man to
> make it over again.'
>
> 'Certainly the Lord made it,' replied Felix, laughing, 'and He
> made it very well. But life has been touching up the work. It is
> a very interesting type of head. It's delightfully wasted and emaci-
> ated. The complexion is wonderfully bleached.' And Felix looked
> round at the circle, as if to call attention to these interesting points.
>
> Mr. Wentworth grew visibly paler.　　　　　Ch. 5, p. 62

I think James means us here to sympathise with Mr. Wentworth
in his witty and dignified resistance—certainly the Europeans
have no monopoly of wit—and perhaps Felix is tainted by his
sister's vulgarity, a vulgarity bred of sophistication; but with
him it's a venial fault, not revealing a serious limitation of
sympathy. Her appreciation, on the other hand, is never truly
disinterested. The following passage suggests the connection
between her aesthetic sense and her self-interest:

> She was capable of enjoying anything that was characteristic,
> anything that was good of its kind—the Wentworth household
> seemed to her very perfect of its kind, wonderfully peaceful and
> unspotted; pervaded by a sort of dove-coloured freshness that had
> all the quietude and benevolence of what she deemed to be Quaker-
> ism, and yet seemed to be founded upon a degree of material abun-
> dance for which, in certain matters of detail, one might have
> looked in vain at the frugal little court of Silberstadt-Schreckenstein.
> She perceived immediately that her American relatives thought and
> talked very little about money; and this of itself made an impression

upon Eugenia's imagination. She perceived at the same time that if Charlotte or Gertrude should ask their father for a very considerable sum he would at once place it in their hands; and this made a still greater impression.

Ch. 4, p. 51

'. . . anything that was characteristic, anything that was good of its kind'; this sort of judging works well enough for things, but not for people. Her appreciation of the wealth, and the women's access to it, is made by comparison with Europe. A few pages later, another passage stresses the importance to her of the comparative standard:

> She knew that she had never been so real a power, never counted for so much, as now when, for the first time, the standard of comparison of her little circle was a prey to vagueness. The sense, indeed, that the good people about her had, as regards her remarkable self, no standard of comparison at all, gave her a feeling of almost illimitable power.
>
> Ch. 4, p. 56

Felix's appreciation, on the other hand, has no strings attached to it: it is both more aesthetic and thereby more generous. This is already implicit in the first chapter when his artist's eye responds to the unfamiliar scene while his sister remains obstinately disgruntled.

All this makes a 'subject' that recurs in many of James's major works: the relation of the aesthetic sense to the moral life. The former can be cultivated in a narrowly materialistic way which leads, in the end, to the tyranny of treating people as objects of use—an outstanding instance of this is Gilbert Osmond in *The Portrait of a Lady*. Yet if it encourages not a competitive spirit but a genuinely disinterested love of the 'otherness' of other things and other people, then the aesthetic sense enhances life. Felix Young, whatever the quality of his painting, is an artist in the art of living. His sister is always *expecting* things from life, and in her different way she fails as signally as the Americans to *enjoy* it. They are inhibited by an over-developed conscience and a social ethos based on high ideals but narrow principles; she is inhibited by too low a view of life—what is she going to get out of America? how can it advance her position?

She appreciates so little, and her comments in private are so frequently derogatory, that the reader is bound to part company with her judgment, and it may well seem that James has weighted the scales too heavily against her and made it incredible that she should so fascinate her cousins. He invokes our sympathy for her threatened marital status and uncertain future, but even her most tender moment is qualified in a most damaging way:

> She kept looking round the circle; she knew that there was admiration in all the eyes that were fixed upon her. She smiled at them all.
> 'I came to look—to try—to ask,' she said. 'It seems to me I have done well. *I am very tired; I want to rest.*' There were tears in her eyes. The luminous interior, the gentle, tranquil people, the simple, serious life—the sense of these things pressed upon her with an overmastering force, and she felt herself yielding to *one of the most genuine emotions she had ever known.* 'I should like to stay here,' she said. 'Pray take me in.'   Ch. 3, p. 42 (My italics)

We first see the Baroness telling lies over small things. A more serious instance occurs when she is visiting Robert Acton's invalid mother:

> 'I have heard a great deal about you,' she said softly, to the Baroness.
> 'From your son, eh?' Eugenia asked. 'He has talked to me immensely of you. Oh, he talks of you as you would like,' the Baroness declared; 'as such a son *must* talk of such a mother!'
> Mrs. Acton sat gazing; this was part of Madame Münster's 'manner'. But Robert Acton was gazing too, in vivid consciousness that he had barely mentioned his mother to their brilliant guest. He never talked of this still maternal presence—a presence refined to such delicacy that it had almost resolved itself, with him, simply into the subjective emotion of gratitude. And Acton rarely talked of his emotions. The Baroness turned her smile toward him, and she instantly felt that she had been observed to be fibbing. She had struck a false note. But who were these people to whom such fibbing was not pleasing?   Ch. 6, p. 84

Here the motive looks respectable, but the intimacy of the subject—the relations of mother and son—makes the compliment a vulgar impertinence. Her insincerity is more attractively and perhaps more subtly embodied in Jane Austen's character Mary Crawford, in *Mansfield Park*. She too comes from outside, from the metropolis into a small provincial circle, and nearly wins a husband there. The Baroness's greater vulgarity is that of a later period and a dubious cosmopolitan sophistication. Mrs. Luna, in *The Bostonians*, is a still more flagrant case.

The details of how things go wrong for the Baroness are a little complicated. I have seen it written that she refuses Robert Acton's proposal of marriage, but what actually happens—at least as I understand it—is more interesting than that. After the falsehood quoted above, Acton is suspicious and he puts her to a test she can't face: he intimates to her that he won't make her an offer until she has first renounced her German husband, for which, as she's told him, she has only to sign and despatch an official document. She won't say whether she has sent it or not, keeping him in suspense in the hope of provoking an explicit offer from him. It doesn't come. Finally, in desperation, she says, falsely, that she's sent it, but by now he doesn't trust her any more, so that even this subterfuge doesn't win him. She meets her match, in subtlety and circumspection, on American soil.

Compared with his later work, this novel is full of critical generalisations about the characters. It would not be absurd to call it a dramatised debate on the relations between duty and pleasure, or between the aesthetic and the moral sense. But this makes the book sound more like a tract than a story, whereas for a number of reasons it's one of the lightest and most readily enjoyable of James's novels.

Firstly, good and bad, the admirable and the ridiculous, are distributed among the characters with a delicate and constantly shifting balance that bears comparison with the greatest comic writers. The novel deals in as brilliant a way as Molière's *Le Misanthrope*, for example, with the way temperament and moral principles combine or conflict, and how the former tends to compromise or undermine the latter. In tragedy, good and bad— or rather, good and evil— have to be more clearly set apart from one another, and we find this in James's more tragic novels, from *The American* and *The Portrait of a Lady* onwards. In the world of *The Europeans* there is no evil, and if there are 'certain stiff barriers' and an absence of joy, there are also some notable liberties: as Felix observes, these American girls are not, like European ones, 'under glass'. And we can see that the liberties depend on the restrictions.

Secondly, there is the happy alliance between James's own moral concern and that of his characters. He has found for them a style of speech in which to discuss serious matters with the brevity of wit. The plot is forwarded by means of dialogue rather than narrative, so that it reads like a series of scenes between different pairs of characters, with an occasional larger grouping, and the conversations are often neatly rounded off in a way that recalls a scene in a good comedy. Here is Felix courting Gertrude Wentworth:

'I shall never marry Mr. Brand,' she said.

'I see!' Felix rejoined. And they slowly descended the hill together, saying nothing till they reached the margin of the pond. 'It is your own affair,' he then resumed; 'but do you know, I am not altogether glad? If it were settled that you were to marry Mr. Brand I should take a certain comfort in the arrangement, I should feel more free. I have no right to make love to you myself, eh?' And he paused, lightly pressing his argument upon her.

'None whatever,' replied Gertrude quickly—too quickly.

'Your father would never hear of it; I haven't a penny. Mr. Brand, of course, has property of his own, eh?'

'I believe he has some property; but that has nothing to do with it.'

'With you, of course not; but with your father and sister it must have. So, as I say, if this were settled, I should feel more at liberty.'

'More at liberty?' Gertrude repeated. 'Please unfasten the boat.'

Felix untwisted the rope and stood holding it. 'I should be able to say things to you that I can't give myself the pleasure of saying now,' he went on. 'I could tell you how much I admire you, without seeming to pretend to that which I have no right to pretend to. I should make violent love to you,' he added laughing, 'if I thought you were so placed as not to be offended by it.'

'You mean if I were engaged to another man? That is strange reasoning!' Gertrude exclaimed.

'In that case you would not take me seriously.'

'I take every one seriously!' said Gertrude. And without his help she stepped lightly into the boat.   Ch. 7, p. 99

Then there is the neatness of the plot with its balancing pairs of characters all held slightly at a distance from the reader and not, as in tragedy, with one central character who suffers his soul to be laid bare. And although the Baroness fails to find a husband, the shifting balance of the pairs finally resolves itself, as romantic comedy should, into a number of marriages.

Finally, there is the pastoral scene, traditional setting for the raising of questions about the nature of the good life. Over it even the Baroness casts a benevolent eye:

> It seemed to her, when . . . she looked out over the soundless fields, the stony pastures, the clear-faced ponds, the rugged little orchards, that she had never been in the midst of so peculiarly intense a stillness; it was almost a delicate sensual pleasure. It was all very good, very innocent and safe, and out of it something good must come.
>
> Ch. 4, p. 51

There is even a suggestion of the ancient connection between comedy and the rhythm of the seasonal year. The novel opens with winter having a final fling, though 'the blessed vernal season is already six weeks old'; but later that day 'The sun broke out through the snow-clouds and jumped into the Baroness's room . . . From one hour to another the day had grown vernal; even in the bustling streets there was an odour of earth and blossom.' 'The next day', when Felix enters the pastoral scene, 'was splendid . . . If the winter had suddenly leaped into spring, the spring had for the moment as quickly leaped into summer.' Much later on, outdoors with Gertrude in the still perfect summer weather,

> Felix spoke at last, in the course of talk, of his going away; it was the first time he had alluded to it.
>
> 'You are going away?' said Gertrude, looking at him.
>
> 'Some day—when the leaves begin to fall. You know I can't stay for ever.'

> Gertrude transferred her eyes to the outer prospect, and then, after a pause, she said, 'I shall never see you again.'
>
> Ch. 7, p. 95

The circle is complete. These are small touches, but they evoke memories of other stories, and the idyllic quality of the novel would be less marked without them.

Technically, one of the novel's most impressive passages is the few pages at the beginning of Chapter 4, referred to above, which relate the Wentworths' discussion of how they shall house their visitors. Six characters take part in a conversation that really helps to define them all. The scene is forwarding the action, of course, but the characters are given time just to be themselves as well. A comparison with Chapter 12 of *Emma*, which performs a similar function, might help to define James's art. What he doesn't offer is Jane Austen's brilliant differentiation of each character by their style of speech, and here we touch on one of his permanent limitations: his characters rarely have that strong individuality of utterance which gives to those of Dickens, for example, even more obviously than to Jane Austen's, a memorable life of their own quite apart from what happens to them. Perhaps James's wandering life gave him no chance of getting to know a single society inside out and thus gaining a sure enough grasp of its linguistic range to enable him to use it creatively in this way; or perhaps, if he had given his characters a more realistically idiosyncratic speech, they would not have been fit spokesmen of the ideas he wanted them to express. These questions are easier to raise than to answer.

3

Washington Square (1880)

This story could have been very sentimental. A plain, intensely humble girl is courted by an unscrupulous adventurer for the sake of her money. Deceived by his professions of love, she loves him in return. Her clear-sighted father, whom she adores, sees through the young man's pretensions and determines to discourage the match. He ruthlessly exploits his influence over his daughter and eventually succeeds, at the expense of forfeiting her trust in himself. Her lover jilts her and she is left alone, her affections betrayed, to finish her days in isolation.

It certainly sounds like a sad story, and there were precedents in Victorian fiction for a straightforward sentimental treatment. James's handling of it is neither sentimental nor straightforward. Sentimentality is superficial, but he makes the surface of his narrative too comic for it to gain a footing; and he penetrates the psychology of his heroine's struggles so that they become intensely dramatic, and mere pathos is out of the question.

There were precedents in literature, from the lives of the saints onwards, for having a humble heroine, but perhaps none in the history of the novel for a heroine who is neither beautiful, high-spirited, specially intelligent, nor merely exemplary in her virtue. Chaucer's *Clerk's Tale* has a heroine who mostly suffers in silence, but once you set the two stories side by side the differences are more striking than the resemblances. Grisilde simply obeys and suffers, and is thus an ideal example of certain Christian virtues. There is little psychological interest; she simply *is* a good, that is to say an obedient, wife. James's heroine, on the other hand, experiences 'a great excitement in trying to be a good daughter'. Grisilde gives up her children meekly, but Catherine fights for her lover, and James explores the limits of her submission. Grisilde's trials and reward are spectacular. Catherine's trials involve only the cruelty of words and silence—she is, as the narrator points out, 'completely divested of the characteristics of a victim'—and in the end her reward, such as it is, is to have survived her deprivations without prejudice to her integrity. She has a lonely life, and as those nearest to her each in turn betray her in their different ways, her loneliness increases. She survives not by divine grace, but by a unique mixture of humility, simplicity, honesty, patience, good faith, obstinacy, intuition and residual pride. These qualities make up the portrait of a nature that, in its own peculiar way, is morally healthy and strong. And to her moral strength corresponds a physical stamina which James repeatedly emphasises.

Catherine maintains or recovers what Jane Austen's heroines call their 'tranquillity' and what James refers to on one occasion as her 'self-possession'. It is an ancient ideal, aristocratic rather than Christian. Socrates puts it like this in *The Republic*: 'We reckon that the good man's life is the most complete in itself and least dependent on others. So the loss of son or brother, or of property or whatever, will hold the least terrors for the good man, who, when some such catastrophe overtakes him, will mourn it less and bear it more calmly than others.' Catherine herself does not recognise it as an ideal, but when the classic solutions of romance—passionate fulfilment, sacrifice, abandonment to the will of another—are denied her, this is what she falls back on, and the reader can see that her whole life has been a training in this unromantic virtue. That she instinctively grasps its importance is nicely shown when after a sleepless night she insists on going down to breakfast as usual, though her aunt protests that she is throwing away a great opportunity:

'You should not go to breakfast,' she said; 'you are not well enough, after your fearful night.'
'Yes, I am very well, and I am only afraid of being late.'
'I can't understand you,' Mrs. Penniman cried. 'You should stay in bed for three days.'

'Oh, I could never do that,' said Catherine, to whom this idea presented no attractions.

Mrs. Penniman was in despair; and she noted, with extreme annoyance, that the trace of the night's tears had completely vanished from Catherine's eyes. She had a most impracticable physique. 'What effect do you expect to have upon your father,' her aunt demanded, 'if you come plumping down, without a vestige of any sort of feeling, as if nothing in the world had happened?'

'He would not like me to lie in bed,' said Catherine simply.

'All the more reason for your doing it. How else do you expect to move him?'

Catherine thought a little. 'I don't know how; but not in that way. I wish to be just as usual.'   Ch. 19, p. 95

Scene after scene in the novel shows her subjected to the unreasonable demands of others, and gradually she attains the moral poise to resist and even to answer back. Her firmness of tone with her aunt, on her return from Europe, is thus a convincing development:

'Nothing is changed—nothing but my feeling about father. I don't mind nearly so much now. I have been as good as I could, but he doesn't care. Now I don't care either. I don't know whether I have grown bad; perhaps I have. But I don't care for that. I have come home to be married—that's all I know.'   Ch. 25, p.124

The last two or three chapters, which carry us on some twenty years past 'the season of her misery', clarify the conditions of Catherine's survival: the resistance to change, the habits 'rather stiffly maintained', the refusal of other, more eligible suitors. When Morris intrudes once again on her privacy she makes 'the strangest observation. It seemed to be he, and yet not he; it was the man who had been everything, and yet this person was nothing. How long ago it was—how old she had grown—how much she had lived. She had lived on something that was connected with *him*, and she had consumed it in doing so' (Ch. 35). To say that she has remained true to the memory, the idea, of her lover would be to oversimplify the subtle point of that last sentence.

The Doctor, her father, 'so sure that he was right', is one of many portraits in James of the 'strong' character whose strength is bound up with his limitations. He is strong because he sees life in clear but oversimplified terms. He is right most of the time, and about most of the other characters, but he completely misjudges his daughter. After his wife's death his only child should have been his closest tie, but he decides, prematurely, that she will never develop into the sort of woman he could be proud of, and he adopts a sarcastic, patronising manner towards her which keeps her at an awestruck distance and ensures that she continues to appear to him what he has decided she must be. Her birth was the occasion of his wife's death, and the Doctor's resentment of this circumstance provides, if we want it, a psychological explanation of the way he treats his daughter. This point, barely hinted in the early pages, is left by James to be brought into the open by Catherine herself, at one of those moving moments late in the story when, under the pressure of distress, her maturing judgment expresses what she has long dumbly felt: 'He is not very fond of me . . . He can't help it . . . It's because he is so fond of my mother, whom we lost so long ago. She was beautiful, and very, very brilliant; he is always thinking of her. I am not at all like her' (Ch. 26).

Like the narrator, the Doctor is a witty man and expresses himself frequently in an ironical form. Here is his tone:

> 'Of course I wish Catherine to be good . . . but she won't be any the less virtuous for not being a fool. I am not afraid of her being wicked; she will never have the salt of malice in her character. She is 'as good as good bread', as the French say; but six years hence I don't want to have to compare her to good bread-and-butter.'
>
> Ch. 2, p. 10

In reporting the Doctor's thoughts James can use his normal narrative style—shapely syntax, ironic inflation of vocabulary, cool urbanity—without any effect of incongruity. Their common style suggests a common point of view, and the Doctor being obviously the cleverest character in the book, the reader must feel some inclination to identify with him. Yet he is a tyrant who treats his daughter with abominable cruelty, and a sarcastic irony is one of his sharpest weapons against her. As the story unfolds we have to dissociate ourselves more and more from his point of view. His cruelty to Catherine turns out to be quite superfluous in preventing the marriage, and the struggle between them, in which the strength and initiative seem always to be on his side, ends in victory for neither. Ironically, in resisting her father Catherine develops a strength and obstinacy like his own. He meets his match in her, and both are frustrated—Catherine of her lover, and the Doctor of any acknowledgement from her that she has given her lover up or that he was right to obstruct the match. He doesn't even know for certain that the two aren't still in league and lying low till he dies. His punishment, therefore, is that he must maintain to the end of his days that haughty distrust that once seemed appropriate. Like one of the damned in Dante's *Inferno*, he is fixed in the attitude that exemplifies his sin.

The struggle between these two central characters directly involves two others whose duplicity or stupidity invites our contempt. James's comic treatment of them, which is partly based on their efforts to play the traditional roles of romantic lover and heroine's confidante, seasons our contempt with laughter. The more obviously comic of the two is Catherine's Aunt Lavinia, Mrs. Penniman, who takes a romantic interest in her niece's love affair and whose 'meddlesome folly' and 'blundering alacrity' protract her ordeal.

> Mrs. Penniman delighted of all things in a drama, and she flattered herself that a drama would now be enacted. Combining as she did the zeal of the prompter with the impatience of the spectator, she had long since done her utmost to pull up the curtain. She, too, expected to figure in the performance—to be the confidante, the Chorus, to speak the epilogue. It may even be said that there were times when she lost sight altogether of the modest heroine of the play in the contemplation of certain great scenes which would naturally occur between the hero and herself.   Ch. 10, p. 50

Mrs. Penniman's view of life is highly coloured by notions of romance and drama, and James here develops the analogy in a virtuoso manner and at ridiculous length. The virtuosity is not Mrs. Penniman's but it suits her exuberant imagination, and after the second sentence, unflattering to her dignity, the passage rises to a level that she would probably consider not far beneath her own. Yet in another way the passage is not fanciful at all: it sums up accurately the part that Mrs. Penniman is indeed going to play in the story, and its details are exemplified by the subsequent action.

In showing how Mrs. Penniman's sentimental interest gradually shifts from Catherine to Morris, James makes a splendid study of a kind of unconscious emotional dishonesty, quite different from the calculated dishonesty of the young man, but in its way disastrous—as when she unconsciously betrays Catherine to Morris: 'Mr. Townsend . . . shall I tell you something? She loves you so much that you may do anything . . . You may postpone—you may change about; she won't think the worse of you' (Ch. 21). Some of the funniest passages in the book are the confabulations of these two:

> 'I have something very important to tell you.'
> 'Well, let's have it,' said Morris.
> 'I was perhaps a little headlong the other day in advising you to marry immediately. I have been thinking it over, and now I see it just a little differently.'
> 'You seem to have a great many ways of seeing the same object.'
> 'Their number is infinite!' said Mrs. Penniman, in a tone which seemed to suggest that this convenient faculty was one of her brightest attributes.
> 'I recommend you to take one way and stick to it,' Morris replied.
> 'Ah, but it isn't easy to choose. My imagination is never quiet, never satisfied. It makes me a bad adviser, but it makes me a capital friend.'
> 'A capital friend who gives bad advice!' said Morris.
> 'Not intentionally—and who hurries off, at every risk, to make the most humble excuses.'
> 'Well, what do you advise me now?'
> 'To be very patient; to watch and wait.'
> 'And is that bad advice or good?'

The consistently comic treatment of Mrs. Penniman serves to
define by contrast the heroine and her tragic possibilities: it
highlights her aunt's stupid dishonesty, and against it we appreciate that Catherine is extremely honest and, in an important
respect, intelligent, though no one gives her credit for it. Above
all, the treatment of Mrs. Penniman is anti-romantic, in the
tradition of *Northanger Abbey:* it exposes her inveterate desire
to doll things up and give herself a picturesque role to play.
Repeatedly, her distorted view of people and events prompts
the reader to realise their actually quite humble and prosaic
qualities, and this gives them a dignity more eloquent than
direct assertion could achieve.

The narrative enters less into the consciousness of Morris Townsend than into that of the other principal characters. His function
is chiefly to be, in words and actions, a specious but spurious
version of what Catherine takes him for. He has to act a part in
her eyes—the fond and disinterested lover—and he does it well
enough to deceive her. He also acts a part in the eyes of Mrs.
Penniman, but Mrs. Penniman writes it for him, and the effort
required from him is minimal. His interest as a character is not
a psychological one: it lies in the way he sustains these roles,
and the gap between them and the truth about him is a source of
ironic comedy. At his first appearance James indicates by stylistic
means the kind of interest the reader is to take in him. He and
Catherine have just met at a party. They dance, and then sit down
together:

> Catherine leaned back in her place, with her eyes fixed upon him,
> smiling, and thinking him very clever. He had features like young
> men in pictures; Catherine had never seen such features—so
> delicate, so chiselled and finished—among the New Yorkers whom
> she passed in the streets and met at dancing-parties. He was tall and
> slim, but he looked extremely strong. Catherine thought he looked
> like a statue. But a statue would not talk like that, and, above all,
> would not have eyes of so rare a colour. He had never been at
> Mrs. Almond's before; he felt very much like a stranger; and it was

very kind of Catherine to take pity on him. He was Arthur Townsend's cousin—not very near; several times removed—and Arthur had brought him to present him to the family. In fact, he was a great stranger in New York. It was his native place; but he had not been there for many years. He had been knocking about the world, and living in queer corners; he had only come back a month or two before. New York was very pleasant, only he felt lonely.

'You see, people forget you,' he said, smiling at Catherine with his delightful gaze, while he leaned forward obliquely, turning towards her, with his elbows on his knees.　　　　Ch. 4, p. 19

This passage begins as narration from Catherine's point of view; it tells us what she is thinking and feeling. Then, halfway through, with the words 'He had never been at Mrs. Almond's before', it moves without warning into a kind of indirect or reported speech. The young man's words are incorporated into the narrative, not recorded directly as dialogue. What is the point of presenting his speech in this form? By telescoping into one paragraph remarks which must have been strung out between pauses and answers from Catherine, it economises in space without losing the flavour of direct speech. Moreover, those features of the speech which are below the style of the narrative or in some other way characteristic of the speaker show up the more clearly; the absence of inverted commas leaves to the reader the job of registering the discrepancy. 'It was very kind of Catherine to take pity on him'—this flatters her with the inflated vocabulary of courtly love. 'He was a great stranger in New York'—this is more than the statement of fact that 'a *complete* stranger' would have been. 'Knocking about the world, and living in queer corners'—here self-depreciation, through the undignified colloquialisms, goes with romantic suggestions of adventure and wild oats. And finally: 'He felt lonely'—this combines with 'a great stranger' to solicit her sympathy, but strikes too personal and intimate a note not to be suspect in a first conversation with a young girl. If Morris were going to be the hero of the story this would be an undignified way to treat his first speech of any length. Unobtrusively it puts us on our guard and draws attention to what is suspicious about him. At this point, indeed, we already have to part company with the heroine, whose impressions of him are wholly favourable.

James reverts to narrative:

> They sat there for some time. He was very amusing. He asked her about the people that were near them; he tried to guess who some of them were, and he made the most laughable mistakes. He criticised them very freely, in a positive, off-hand way.

The narrative here is interspersed with straightforward comments from Catherine's point of view: 'He was very amusing', 'the most laughable mistakes', 'very freely, in a positive, off-hand way'. Although we are not explicitly told so, we register these phrases as an account of how it strikes *her*, and, without actually dissociating ourselves from her impressions, we reserve judgment, made aware of the possibility of error by what has gone before and what we already know of her limited powers. What follows takes us right inside her consciousness:

> Catherine had never heard anyone—especially any young man—talk just like that. It was the way a young man might talk in a novel; or, better still, in a play, on the stage, close before the footlights, looking at the audience, and with everyone looking at him, so that you wondered at his presence of mind. And yet Mr. Townsend was not like an actor; he seemed so sincere, so natural.

There is no explicit introductory formula like 'She thought that...' or 'She said to herself...', but there is no doubt these are her thoughts. 'He seemed so sincere, so natural'; this naïve and enthusiastic judgment is a long way from the narrator's habitual ironic tones. (Catherine is incapable of irony.) And there are other stylistic indications, such as the loosely-knit syntax—'in a play, on the stage, close before the footlights, looking at the audience, and with everyone looking at him, so that you wondered at his presence of mind'—which suggests the way Catherine rather slowly fits the bits of her picture together. The narrator's syntax never has this slackness.

The passage tells us something important about Catherine: she finds Morris Townsend convincing—and were she not to cling to this impression with devoted obstinacy there would be no story. How much more dramatic that this information should be given 'subjectively', through her consciousness—it has the pulse of life. What complicates the situation with a fine irony is that she is convinced by him in spite of recognising some of the truth about him: he *is* talking to her like a young man in a novel, or a play, and her perception of this is expressed in words that catch the naïve wonderment of a young girl's first critical reflections on the art of coarse acting.

In a normal reading there is no call for the reader to take conscious note, as I have tried to do, of these shifts of style and point of view. Nevertheless he must in some way register them if he is to read with full comprehension. Broadly speaking, their effect is a comic one; they require the reader frequently and nimbly to adjust his point of view and they give the surface of the narrative a sparkling diversity.

The action is virtually confined to these four characters. There is also one minor character of importance, the Doctor's other sister, Mrs. Almond. With her he discusses his daughter's affair at regular intervals throughout the story, and she represents the combination of intelligence and sympathy that we look for in vain in any of the three major characters surrounding the heroine. Her wit matches her brother's, and sometimes has the same Gallic touch. When Mrs. Penniman insists that Morris will make Catherine 'a lovely husband':

> 'I don't believe in lovely husbands,' said Mrs. Almond; 'I only believe in good ones.' Ch. 23, p. 114

This is in similar style to La Rochefoucauld's maxim: 'Il y a de bons mariages, mais il n'y en a point de délicieux.'

When the Doctor dismisses Catherine as 'absolutely unattractive ... neither pretty nor lively', we know that he voices the common judgment of society, measuring the individual case by applying conventional standards. It is a simple operation that involves no imagination, no appreciation of his daughter for what she is in herself, or might become. (Catherine has felt the full weight of its authority, as we see when, with disarming honesty, she wishes to have it recognised between her lover and herself: 'You know how little there is in me to be proud of. I am ugly and stupid.') Mrs. Almond's reply to the Doctor gives another view which is both sympathetic, realistic and disinterested:

> 'Catherine does very well; she has a style of her own—which is more than my poor Marian has, who has no style at all,' said Mrs. Almond. 'The reason Catherine has received so little attention, is that she seems to all the young men to be older than themselves. She is so large, and she dresses so richly. They are rather afraid of her, I think; she looks as if she had been married already, and you know they don't like married women ... Wait till some intelligent man of forty comes along, and he will be delighted with Catherine.' Ch. 6, p. 34

Mrs. Almond is a minor character, hardly more than a voice, but a voice whose superior style gives it a special authority. When the Doctor, in his last scene with her, dismisses Catherine's heart-breaking experience:

> 'She hasn't much to say; but when had she anything to say? She had her little dance, and now she is sitting down to rest. I suspect that, on the whole, she enjoys it.'

Mrs. Almond replies:

> 'She enjoys it as people enjoy getting rid of a leg that has been crushed. The state of mind after amputation is doubtless one of comparative repose.'

The shocking analogy is well chosen for someone of her brother's profession; but he doesn't recognise the heart's reasons and neatly turns the point:

> 'If your leg is a metaphor for young Townsend, I can assure you he has never been crushed ...' Ch. 32, p.158

Washington Square is not, like *The Europeans*, full of ideas. It is the story of a life, and when we finish it, it seems complete and fully treated, for all its shortness. This is because the most significant action of that life is concentrated in the space of a few months. James presents that action in a series of unusually short chapters. The story seems to move quickly, and there is a happy balance between narrative and dialogue. The former, urbanely elegant, maintains an ironic detachment from the events, which are set back some forty or fifty years from the time of writing. It presents New York in the 1830s as a society likely to strike the cosmopolitan reader as decidedly provincial. At the same time descriptions of manners and places are affectionately nostalgic—this was the New York of James's own childhood.

Framed by the narrative, dialogue brings the action before us as drama. The scenes are carefully shaped. It is worth studying, for example, how James organises the important scene between the lovers in Chapter 20 so as to exhibit dramatically, that is to say through dialogue which expresses a continual shifting of attitudes, all the facets of the changing situation. The scene begins with Morris urging an immediate union ('Will you marry me tomorrow?') and Catherine holding back ('Isn't it better to wait?'). Then Catherine reveals that her father will disinherit her if she marries without his consent. She realises that her father thinks this will put Morris off, but she doesn't think so herself, and of course Morris cannot admit that the money is what he cares about. All he can do for the moment is to make the idea of disinheritance look suitably awful in her eyes, and suggest at the same time that she might perhaps bring her father round. But he miscalculates his effect: she is more frightened than encouraged, and the ironic consequence is that she is suddenly ready to grant his request for an immediate marriage, though by now he no longer wants it:

> The mortal chill of her situation struck more deeply into her child-like heart, and she was overwhelmed by a feeling of loneliness and danger. But her refuge was there, close to her, and she put out her hands to grasp it. 'Ah, Morris,' she said, with a shudder, 'I will marry you as soon as you please!' and she surrendered herself, leaning her head on his shoulder.
>
> 'My dear good girl!' he exclaimed, looking down at his prize. And then he looked up again, rather vaguely, with parted lips and lifted eyebrows.　　　　　　　　　　　　　　Ch. 20, p. 101

In four pages there has been a reversal of the situation between them, but it has been accomplished so unobtrusively and convincingly that the reader hardly registers it as such. This is as it should be: we must share with Catherine all the other ideas and emotions that occur on the way and cover the bare bones of what is happening. Yet on re-reading we can afford to notice how James has conceived the scene so as to give it this clear dramatic outline. There is a great deal of such unobtrusive artistry in the construction of this novel; not surprisingly, it has been successfully adapted for the stage. The book is a small masterpiece, and it beautifully exemplifies what James himself wrote three years later in his essay on 'The Art of Fiction' (1884):

> I cannot imagine composition existing in a series of blocks, nor conceive, in any novel worth discussing at all, of a passage of description that is not in its intention narrative, a passage of dialogue that is not in its intention descriptive, a touch of truth of any sort that does not partake of the nature of incident, or an incident that derives its interest from any other source than the general and only source of the success of a work of art—that of being illustrative. A novel is a living thing, all one and continuous, like any other organism, and in proportion as it lives will it be found, that in each of the parts there is something of each of the other parts . . .

4

The Portrait of a Lady (1881)

This is the longest of James's novels, running to some six hundred pages. It is commonly reckoned one of his greatest works, and many would say it is his masterpiece. What is the book about? The title suggests the importance of the central character, and James tells us in his preface that he began not with the plot but with the vision of 'a certain young woman affronting her destiny', and that she was vivid to him 'while she stood there in perfect isolation', long before he settled down to 'organising an ado' about her. So the book is about Isabel Archer, an American girl who comes to Europe and makes a bad marriage; and her story is the portrait of a lady. More generally, it is about Americans in Europe: how Europe strikes them, how they resist or conform to European standards of behaviour and morality, how Europe can be for them an education, and a prison. It is about love and marriage and the position of women, in the most sophisticated international society of the late 19th century. It is about the love of style and the desire that life shall be beautiful, and the limitations and corruptions of that desire.

Most comprehensively, it is about freedom. How free was a young girl, beautiful, intelligent and rich, in such a world at such a time? Free her *from* the limits of a particular society and its standards, from material wants, from the need of a husband to support her, multiply the exemptions and the opportunities, and then see what she will use her freedom *for*. Will it be a grand thing that such a creature, high-spirited and high-principled, be able thoroughly to 'meet the requirements of her imagination'? Can such a girl be 'as good as her best opportunities'? Or is such an exemption from the common necessities of life not a benefit but a burden? Will it lead her into traps that would never have waylaid her if she had stayed at home? Is such a conception of freedom altogether an illusion, and will her course therefore be one of tragic disillusionment?

The book raises such questions, often explicitly in the words and thoughts of the characters. Thus Isabel repeatedly asserts her liberty, or at least her desire for liberty, as a general point in the middle of a particular discussion:

> 'You've lately lost your father?' ...
>
> 'Yes; more than a year ago. After that my aunt was very kind to me; she came to see me and proposed that I should come with her to Europe.'
>
> 'I see,' said Ralph. 'She has adopted you.'
>
> 'Adopted me?' The girl stared, and her blush came back to her, together with a momentary look of pain which gave her interlocutor some alarm. He had underestimated the effect of his words ... 'Oh no; she has not adopted me. I'm not a candidate for adoption.'
>
> 'I beg a thousand pardons,' Ralph murmured. 'I meant—I meant—' He hardly knew what he meant.
>
> 'You meant she has taken me up. Yes; she likes to take people up. She has been very kind to me; but,' she added with a certain visible eagerness of desire to be explicit, 'I'm very fond of my liberty.'
>
> Ch. 2, p. 20

The conversation is then interrupted, but the theme has been sounded at her first appearance; and the way she brings it up characterises her self-consciousness, her assertiveness, her fear of misunderstanding, her youthful anxiety not only to be serious but to be taken seriously. And the whole thing is built on a verbal quibble, the difference in meaning between 'adopting' someone and 'taking them up'. This is only possible because of the vagueness of the two expressions ('He hardly knew what he meant'): Ralph uses the word 'adopted' loosely, with an intention of humorous exaggeration, but Isabel is an orphan and the word grates on her sense of independence, so she substitutes an even vaguer idiom.

This sort of vagueness, and the verbal play the characters consciously make with it, is a constant and peculiar feature of

James's work. You will not find it, except as a special effect, in earlier fiction. There, words are firm ground: the characters know what they mean in using them and expect to be understood. If one character misunderstands another, it marks a difference in background or intelligence. James's characters also mean to be understood, but their meaning is often so vague as to invite misunderstanding, and they are aware of this. It's not that they are incompetent at expressing themselves. Clarity is difficult for them partly because they live in a world in which standards of behaviour are more uncertain than they used to be, and the language of judgment has become vaguer in consequence—vaguer, for example, than in the smaller world of Jane Austen, where an ideal clarity about standards is expressed in the vocabulary of those characters of whom the author approves. In this respect James is a realist and his work is true to the times he lived in. His own cosmopolitan life no doubt gave him greater insight into this tendency of the age, and the uncertainty is an important aspect of the 'mixture of manners' which is a central interest of his international fictions. But James's characters, or at least the more intelligent of them, are not just the victims of a new uncertainty. It certainly makes life difficult for them, but the best of them see the difficulty as a challenge, even an increment of liberty. Isabel provides a small instance of this in her reaction to discovering that in Europe a young girl is not expected to sit up alone with gentlemen. Having yielded to her aunt's insistence that they retire together, she inquires:

'Wasn't it proper I should remain in the drawing-room?'

'Not in the least. Young girls here—in decent houses—don't sit alone with the gentlemen late at night.'

'You were very right to tell me then,' said Isabel. 'I don't understand it, but I'm very glad to know it.'

'I shall always tell you,' her aunt answered, 'whenever I see you taking what seems to me too much liberty.'

'Pray do; but I don't say I shall always think your remonstrance just.'

'Very likely not. You're too fond of your own ways.'

'Yes, I think I'm very fond of them. But I always want to know the things one shouldn't do.'

'So as to do them?' asked her aunt.

'So as to choose,' said Isabel.   Ch. 7, p. 68

These words are the more salient for being the last of the chapter.

However, it is not so much by anything they do, as by their mere awareness, the quality of their consciousness, that James's characters rise above the modern uncertainty about the significance of words and actions. They face it and sound it out; sometimes playfully, taking delight in the multiplication of ambiguities; sometimes more seriously, when more is at stake, but still with that delight in the play of intelligence which marks them as high-spirited and superior to their fate.

One difference between the earlier and the later works is that in the former the play of ambiguity is mostly confined to lighter moments, while in the latter it abounds throughout. *The Portrait of a Lady* is an early work, but the conversation between Mr. Touchett, Ralph and Lord Warburton in its first chapter, apparently about nothing in particular, is an excellent instance of this aspect of James. The theme of liberty is not explicitly sounded, but the quality of the talk with its plays on words and other jokes, its recognition of unexplored possibilities, its suggestions thrown out and not taken up, the intrusion of general ideas and large doubts, above all the critical self-consciousness of the speakers, gives a lively impression of a sophisticated atmosphere in which questions of behaviour and style of life, and also questions of deeper philosophical import, will naturally arise. Such passages could not have been written by a less cosmopolitan writer. The recognition that social and political change is imminent, and the feeling that life is more complicated for the younger generation, are further elements that give them a moral atmosphere not unlike that of Chekhov's plays, written some fifteen or twenty years later; but James's characters are less conditioned by circumstance than Chekhov's, and their conversation, partly as a consequence, is wittier and more urbane. The book is full of ideas, and in the tone of such passages James has created a medium in which they can float lightly and easily, without drawing too much attention to themselves.

One of the most interesting conversations of a philosophical nature is the one in Chapter 19 in which Isabel and Madame Merle discuss the significance of material possessions. It crops up in a natural way in its context, and James is careful not to carry it so far that we lose sight of the speakers. The ideas are strictly relevant, both as characterising the speakers and as focusing attention on a point at which the issue of liberty crosses with that of style and aesthetic sensibility:

> 'I don't care anything about his house,' said Isabel.
>
> 'That's very crude of you. When you've lived as long as I you'll see that every human being has his shell and that you must take the shell into account. By the shell I mean the whole envelope of circumstances. There's no such thing as an isolated man or woman; we're each of us made up of some cluster of appurtenances. What shall we call our 'self'? Where does it begin? Where does it end? It overflows into everything that belongs to us—and then it flows back again. I know a large part of myself is in the clothes I choose to wear. I've a great respect for *things*! One's self—for other people—is one's expression of one's self; and one's house, one's furniture, one's garments, the books one reads, the company one keeps—these things are all expressive.'
>
> This was very metaphysical . . . Isabel was fond of metaphysics, but was unable to accompany her friend into this bold analysis of the human personality. 'I don't agree with you. I think just the other way. I don't know whether I succeed in expressing myself, but I know that nothing else expresses me. Nothing that belongs to me is any measure of me; everything's on the contrary a limit, a barrier, and a perfectly arbitrary one. Certainly the clothes which, as you say, I choose to wear, don't express me; and heaven forbid they should!'
>
> 'You dress very well,' Madame Merle lightly interposed.
>
> 'Possibly; but I don't care to be judged by that. My clothes may express the dressmaker, but they don't express me. To begin with it's not my own choice that I wear them; they're imposed on me by society.'

> 'Should you prefer to go without them?' Madame Merle in-
> quired in a tone which virtually terminated the discussion.
>
> Ch. 19, p. 201

This is an old question. Madame Merle's view has affiliations with conservatism, classicism, pessimism, paganism; it is the realist and, in the Jamesian context, the European view, while Isabel's is romantic, optimistic, Christian, idealist and, in the Jamesian context, American. It is an important disagreement in the context, since Isabel is going to marry a man who not only takes the opposite view from hers but will try to violate her 'self' and make it, together with his other appurtenances, expressive of his own. The two views do not represent an absolute alternative; both speakers have some right on their side. Isabel would escape from limits by denying them, whereas truly they can be transcended only when they are accepted. The function of the novel is to raise the question, but not to answer it dogmatically. It could be said that there's no need for it to be raised so explicitly. In James's later work it wouldn't be: there, general ideas are touched on, if at all, very lightly and obliquely. In the earlier novels they raise their heads from time to time quite openly. The danger of allowing your characters to be explicitly intellectual is that the ideas take over and the character becomes a mere mouthpiece for them. George Eliot, whom James met on several occasions about this time and whose work he much admired, had produced a classic example of this in her novel *Daniel Deronda* (1876). James wrote a brilliant review of it in the form of a conversation, and the story of its heroine, Gwendolen Harleth, has many interesting resemblances to Isabel Archer's. In George Eliot's presentation of Daniel general ideas get out of hand and kill the life of the character, in spite of the author's manifest excitement in him. As James wrote to his brother, 'Daniel Deronda (Dan'l himself) is indeed a dead, though amiable failure'. In his own work he keeps the general ideas under stricter control.

Metaphysical discussion is only one way of raising the question of personal liberty. It is also kept alive by the extraordinary amount of personal speculation in which the characters indulge:

'I judge more than I used to,' [Madame Merle] said to Isabel, 'but it seems to me one has earned the right. One can't judge till one's forty; before that we're too eager, too hard, too cruel, and in addition much too ignorant. I'm sorry for you; it *will* be a long time before you're forty. But every gain's a loss of some kind; I often think that after forty one *can't* really feel. The freshness, the quickness have certainly gone. You'll keep them longer than most people; it will be a great satisfaction to me to see you some years hence. I want to see what life makes of you. One thing's certain— it can't spoil you. It may pull you about horribly, but I defy it to break you up.'   Ch. 19, p. 188

This is a free speculation about possibilities, on a more serious subject, similar to the light-hearted conversation in the first chapter. Such speculation is endemic to James's world: all the major characters indulge in it, and it is a *raison d'être* of those whose role is chiefly a spectator's one. This includes the first-person narrators and third-person observers through whose experience many of the short stories are told, and many major characters in the novels, including Ralph Touchett in this one. Whether or not the speculation is patronising, as it often is with Madame Merle, it's one of the things that make James unreadable for some people. One can see how their objection might be worded: 'These people are the idle rich. They've got nothing serious to do and this is their most sophisticated dissipation: they exercise their fine imaginations in a kind of communal egotism, a discussion of one another that flatters their pride and stimulates their expectations as an antidote to boredom. What else is Madame Merle doing in this passage but encouraging Isabel to find herself and her friend even more interesting than before? They couldn't indulge themselves like this if their time was more usefully employed.' Whether we think their condition blessed or monstrous, James draws out its implications: this is what can happen when intelligent people have such exemptions and opportunities; they are the princes and nobles of the 19th century, who have learned to flatter one another instead of having courtiers and poets do it for them. A sympathetic critic will not be content to lump it all together as idle speculation or

65

reciprocal flattery. Some of James's characters are morally aware of the conditions of freedom and uncertainty in which they live, and can view their opportunities critically: 'We know too much about people in these days,' says Ralph to Isabel; 'we hear too much. Our ears, our minds, our mouths, are stuffed with personalities. Don't mind anything anyone tells you about anyone else. Judge everyone and everything for yourself.'

Isabel, adrift in Europe and suddenly made independent of her relatives by a legacy of seventy thousand pounds, certainly receives a bewildering amount of attention and variety of advice from those around her. Not only where you live and how you live, but the choice of a morality and even the cultivation of a particular consciousness or temperament seem to have become, given the means and the leisure, matters on which to exercise a free choice; and over the whole range of possibilities the famous New England conscience with which James's American heroes and heroines are endowed, hovers anxiously, trying to pick out the one right course. 'You all live here this way,' she says to Edward Rosier of the American colony in Paris, 'but what does it lead to?' And he replies that there is 'nothing for a gentleman in America'. To her cousin Ralph she declares:

> 'I think people suffer too easily . . . It's not absolutely necessary to suffer; we were not made for that.'
> 'You were not, certainly.'
> 'I'm not speaking of myself.' And she wandered off a little.
> 'No, it isn't a fault,' said her cousin. 'It's a merit to be strong.'
> 'Only, if you don't suffer they call you hard,' Isabel remarked.
>
> Ch. 5, p. 48

Yet in refusing Lord Warburton she gives as her reason that 'I can't escape my fate . . . I should try to escape it if I were to marry you . . . I can't escape unhappiness . . . In marrying you I shall be trying to.' A few days later she is refusing Caspar Goodwood, her American suitor, on the grounds that 'I like my liberty too much. . . Besides, I try to judge things for myself . . . I wish to choose my fate.'

66

Behind the wholly convincing inconsistency of her ideas lies a brilliant sketch, in Chapters 3, 4 and 6, of a partly American, partly cosmopolitan upbringing, irregular and peripatetic, which is strongly reminiscent of James's own. The subject of these three chapters is filled in with an amount of detail that makes the rest of the book, as far as physical background goes, look a little thin in comparison. One of Isabel's most suggestive memories (one of James's too?) is of being withdrawn at her own request from the little primary school on the other side of the street from the family house in Albany, and allowed instead to stay at home, 'where, in the September days, when the windows of the Dutch house were open, she used to hear the hum of childish voices repeating the multiplication table—an incident in which the elation of liberty and the pain of exclusion were indistinguishably mingled'. 'The elation of liberty and the pain of exclusion'— the ambiguous emotion, so beautifully focused by the details of the scene, lies at the roots, psychologically, of much that is to follow. Her case resembles that of Jane Austen's Emma: the mother lost in infancy, the indulgent father, the straightforward elder sister who is married, the lack of intellectual discipline, the love of her personal independence, the intelligence and the zest for life.

> Her thoughts were a tangle of vague outlines which had never been corrected by the judgment of people speaking with authority. In matters of opinion she had had her own way, and it had led her into a thousand ridiculous zigzags. At moments she discovered she was grotesquely wrong, and then she treated herself to a week of passionate humility. After this she held her head higher than ever again; for it was of no use, she had an unquenchable desire to think well of herself. Ch. 6, p. 50

All this of Isabel is curiously similar to what Jane Austen tells us of Emma, and each heroine engages our sympathy in spite of, even because of, her presumptuousness. But no sooner has the resemblance been noted than the differences obtrude themselves. Isabel 'was always planning out her development, desiring her perfection, observing her progress'. Then she thinks of 'the thousands of people who were less happy than herself—a thought which for the moment made her fine, full consciousness appear a kind of immodesty. What should one do with the misery of the world in a scheme of the agreeable for oneself?' The little world of Hartfield is large enough for Emma, and no one is moved to leave her a legacy of seventy thousand pounds to 'meet the requirements of her imagination'. The wide horizons which open up before James's heroine bring a concomitant anxiety and insecurity, and as a foundation for these to build upon there is already the exaggerated tension between the conceived demands of duty and pleasure which is a classic feature of the New England conscience, as James had already depicted it in *The Europeans*.

Isabel Archer, with her cosmopolitan upbringing, is not a straightforward New England product, but the Puritan ethos has made its mark upon her: she is in search of justification. However, she is also sensitive, like Gertrude Wentworth, to other values. On one occasion Ralph tells her to 'take things more easily. Don't question your conscience so much—it will get out of tune like a strummed piano. Keep it for great occasions. Don't try so much to form your character—it's like trying to pull open a tight, tender young rose. Live as you like best, and your character will take care of itself . . .' (Ch. 21, p. 222). The voice of Ralph here is the voice of Felix Young in *The Europeans*, and that of Lambert Strether in *The Ambassadors*, in his famous outburst to Little Bilham which, reported to James as that of a Bostonian friend of his, the novelist William Dean Howells, became the seed of anecdote from which that novel sprang: 'Live all you can; it's a mistake not to. It doesn't so much matter what you do in particular, so long as you have your life. If you haven't had that what *have* you had?' Isabel responds immediately, but the other voice, the anxious voice of conscience and duty, is never silent in her for long. She and Lambert Strether are the two characters in James who embody this conflict most completely. They carry on the debate with themselves like a Shakespearean character in soliloquy. When another character expresses one side of it, Isabel responds with one half of herself and resists with the other. A large function of Henrietta Stackpole is to be a more entertaining and dramatic mouthpiece for the voice of conscience than Isabel's own reflections can provide.

Ralph and Henrietta, like Madame Merle, have the leisure to interest themselves in Isabel. Henrietta's interest expresses itself in earnest advice which aspires to influence, and Madame Merle's in what looks like a more detached and generous appreciation. Isabel pays attention to the former and respects it, but the latter is more attractive. For one thing it is a tribute to her own attractiveness; for another it seems to leave its object more at liberty; and for a third it corresponds to a similar propensity in herself. She delights in the strangeness of other people—in her aunt's eccentricity, for example, or Henrietta's representativeness. Isabel's appreciation of other people's 'style' lays her open to be particularly fascinated by Madame Merle, who as well as being a striking figure in herself, encourages Isabel's aesthetic response to others by the success she makes of her own cultivation of that sense:

> She appeared to have in her experience a touchstone for everything, and somewhere in the capacious pocket of her genial memory she would find the key to Henrietta's value. 'That's the great thing,' Isabel solemnly pondered; 'that's the supreme good fortune: to be in a better position for appreciating people than they are for appreciating you.' And she added that such, when one considered it, was simply the essence of the aristocratic situation. In this light, if in none other, one should aim at the aristocratic situation.
>
> Ch. 19, p. 190

This free appreciation of others seems to offer a liberation from the censorious inflexibility of Henrietta and Caspar Goodwood; but she is to discover that such an apparent openness can conceal an egoism far narrower than the more moralistic approach to life from which she has thought to escape.

The aesthetic appreciation of other people connects with the appreciation of beautiful places and works of art which Americans, in James's world, consciously come to Europe to cultivate. In the description of Gardencourt which opens the novel the author assumes that the reader, like his characters, values these things, especially when they express the life of a civilised past. The passage reminds us that works of art have their financial value and may be treated as good or bad bargains; that they are also priceless; that they are things to be lived with as well as admired; that they can promote and enhance privacy. Isabel is destined to be considered as a work of art in these various lights, and to see her step-daughter Pansy similarly treated.

What is difficult to explain, though not to feel, is when an aesthetic response to another person is inadequate or perverse. When Isabel responds to 'that radiance of good feeling and good fare' which surrounds Lord Warburton 'like a zone of fine June weather', or thinks of her aunt as a person whose nature has 'so little surface' that 'nothing tender, nothing sympathetic, had ever had a chance to fasten upon it—no windsown blossom, no familiar softening moss', then we feel no call to dissociate ourselves from her view. But as Isabel is quick to feel, Madame Merle strikes her first really false note of appreciation on the occasion when she brings Isabel and Gilbert Osmond together. Isabel sits very quiet and listens to the others' talk. When Osmond has gone,

> Isabel fully expected her friend would scold her for having been so stupid. But to her surprise that lady, who indeed never fell into the mere matter-of-course, said to her in a few moments: 'You were charming, my dear; you were just as one would have wished you. You're never disappointing.'
>
> A rebuke might possibly have been irritating, though it is much more probable that Isabel would have taken it in good part; but, strange to say, the words that Madame Merle actually used caused her the first feeling of displeasure she had known this ally to excite. 'That's more than I intended,' she answered coldly. 'I'm under no obligation that I know of to charm Mr. Osmond.'
>
> Ch. 23, p. 248

Madame Merle is disagreeable here because she suggests an expectation: aesthetically, Isabel has 'performed', come up to scratch. What makes it worse, in fact slightly sinister and, if we know the story, a moment of dramatic irony, is that Madame Merle is speaking not for herself but for another, adding to her role of connoisseur that of art-dealer.

Isabel later sees Pansy being treated in a similar way by her father: 'Isabel was impressed by Osmond's artistic, the plastic view, as it somehow appeared, of Pansy's innocence—her own appreciation of it being more anxiously moral.'

It is a logical step from the egoism of the aesthetic approach (does the other person *please* you?) to the willingness to exploit others for one's own ends (how can the other person be *made* to please you?). The exploitation of Isabel by Madame Merle and Gilbert Osmond is a large part of the story of the book, and there is much to admire in the way James reveals this process to the reader dramatically, through the incident of scene and dialogue, giving the reader only as much further insight into the situation as is necessary for a critical appreciation of what is happening to the heroine. He also uses imagery to express his own judgment and guide the reader's response. Thus Osmond 'thought Miss Archer sometimes of too precipitate a readiness. It was a pity she had that fault, because if she had not had it she would really have had none; she would have been as smooth to his general need of her as handled ivory to the palm.' Her intelligence 'was to be a silver plate, not an earthen one—a plate that he might heap up with ripe fruits, to which it would give a decorative value, so that talk might become for him a sort of served dessert. He found the silver quality in this perfection in Isabel; he could tap her imagination with his knuckle and make it ring.' When Isabel knows the full extent of the deception practised upon her, these elegant images are replaced by a cruder one: 'She saw . . . the dry staring fact that she had been an applied handled hung-up tool, as senseless and convenient as mere shaped wood and iron.'

What makes the tragedy subtle, profound and exemplary is not the subtlety of the deceivers but the degree to which Isabel consciously lends herself to the process of deceit by understanding and accepting their values in the best possible faith. A fine person with a high degree of self-awareness is afflicted with a fatal blindness. The more she sees, the more interesting her story, but she must not see too much for credibility or for our sympathy. As James says of her, 'The love of knowledge co-existed in her mind with the finest capacity for ignorance.' There is indeed something 'fine' in her capacity for ignorance, and James solves the problem of mixing intelligence and bewilderment in his heroine by making her blindness with regard to Madame Merle and Gilbert Osmond a consequence both of what has gone before and of some of her most admirable qualities. What has gone before, and in particular the attentions she has received from Lord Warburton, has disposed her to fear being drawn into someone else's 'system'. Osmond, in his modesty, seems to have no pretensions to a system; having rejected the world, he wishes only to be fine and private. In Caspar Goodwood she has felt herself threatened not by a 'system' but by strong passion and a strong character that knows too clearly what it wants. Osmond is all discretion and stillness, and his detachment seems a promise of liberty achieved.

Furthermore, she requires little inducement to apply to him the aesthetic criteria that will be most flattering: like a work of classical art he strikes her as all of a piece, consistent and complete in every part, so that 'the movement of a single one of his fingers' produces 'the effect of an expressive gesture'. Then, in what he tells her of himself, he plays upon her generosity with a consummate blend of confidence and mystery, trusting her to imagine good things where she can't see them and anticipating criticism by a studied self-disparagement. Watching Osmond at work, subjecting with a minimum of effort her generous spirit to his mean one, is the drama of a hundred pages in the middle of the story. In subtlety it is matched by Madame Merle's wonderful show of frank thoughtfulness and virtuous calculation, never making the dangerous mistake of pretending to be less circumspect than she really is.

The aesthetic attitude to life which Osmond embodies seems to promise liberty, yet Isabel, 'who has dreamed of freedom and nobleness, who has done, as she believes, a generous, natural, clear-sighted thing, finds herself in reality ground in the very mill of the conventional' (Notebooks, p 15). Osmond seems to stand aloof from the vulgarity of the modern world, loving old things and old forms for the nobleness of life they express:

> How but in custom and in ceremony
> Are innocence and beauty born?
>
> Yeats; A PRAYER FOR MY DAUGHTER

Unconventionally brought up, eager to combine the advantages she has missed with those she has enjoyed, Isabel is well placed to fall under the charm of what he seems to offer: a freedom bounded by ideal constraints freely chosen.

> He had told her he loved the conventional; but there was a sense in which this seemed a noble declaration. In that sense, that of the love of harmony and order and decency and of all the stately offices of life, she went with him freely.   Ch. 42, p. 429

She goes with him freely, but into a prison where he uses convention to enchain her:

> This base, ignoble world, it appeared, was after all what one was to live for; one was to keep it forever in one's eye, in order not to enlighten or convert or redeem it, but to extract from it some recognition of one's own superiority ... There were certain things they must do, a certain posture they must take, certain people they must know and not know. When she saw this rigid system close about her, draped though it was in pictured tapestries, that sense of darkness and suffocation of which I have spoken took possession of her; she seemed shut up with an odour of mould and decay.
>
> Ch. 42, p. 430

Osmond is a powerful portrait of a narcissist. Unable to tolerate her independent moral life because it threatens his supremacy, he shuts out Isabel, and the reader. The fact that we don't enter intimately into their married life is virtually a comment upon it, as it is upon that of Gwendolen and Grandcourt in *Daniel Deronda*.

What brands Osmond unforgettably is the terrible humourlessness of his egotism. This complements his confusion of values, since it is by laughter that we stop ourselves taking small things, and ourselves, too seriously. His lack of humour erects a barrier between him and the author, which explains why he cannot be 'gone behind' for more than a few brief moments. This is not to say that James never takes us inside a character without a sense of humour, but if he does so (as with Olive Chancellor in *The Bostonians*) it must be to comic effect, so that we feel the absurdity of what is in fact a morbid condition. He cannot allow this to happen with Osmond or Madame Merle: the drift of the book is tragic and they who work the evil must remain sinister to the end. Besides, they are not comic figures in the heroine's eyes; on the whole she takes them on their own terms, and we must share her point of view. ' "Poor Osmond, with his old curtains and crucifixes!" the Countess Gemini exclaimed.' That is as close as we get to the relief of laughter.

Madame Merle is the finer of the two, generous in her exertions for her former lover and her child. As the Countess Gemini tells Isabel, 'her grand idea has been to be tremendously irreproachable—a kind of full-blown lily—the incarnation of propriety. She has always worshipped that god'. The greatest moral and aesthetic refinement is put to its service—greater in her case than in Osmond's. She is a more extraordinary character, with whom the reader has a longer and more complicated relationship, discovering her more gradually and sharing more of Isabel's illusions about her. Both of them, as Isabel comes to see, are pitiably deceived in the results of their scheming, though the pity is greater for Madame Merle who, because she still loves him, thinks Osmond better than he is, and thus more worthy of Isabel than he turns out to be.

The truth about her husband and her marriage comes home to Isabel in her lonely vigil by her own fireside in the Palazzo Roccanera, some three years after she has become a wife. (Roccanera means 'Black Rock'; 'merle', in French, means blackbird.) On revising the novel nearly thirty years later, James was particularly pleased with this scene (Ch. 42) and called it in his preface 'obviously the best thing in the book'. He recognised that his heroine's adventures were 'mild' in their 'independence of flood and field, of the moving accident, of battle and murder and sudden death', but saw them as becoming 'the stuff of drama' through the intensity of her vision of them. The scene is, he wrote, but the vigil of searching criticism; but it throws the action further forward than twenty 'incidents' might have done. It was designed to have all the vivacity of incident and all the economy of picture. She sits up, by her dying fire, far into the night, under the spell of recognitions on which she finds the last sharpness suddenly wait. It is a representation simply of her motionlessly *seeing*, and an attempt withal to make the mere still lucidity of her act as 'interesting' as the surprise of a caravan or the identification of a pirate.

His satisfaction is understandable. Isabel's adventures are considerably milder than those of George Eliot's Gwendolen Harleth, with whom Isabel is often compared. George Eliot introduces more 'machinery' into her story, multiplying the vicissitudes of her heroine—such things as the financial crash that impoverishes Mrs. Davilow, Mrs. Glasher's dramatic intervention to inform Gwendolen of Grandcourt's illegitimate children, the arrival of the jewels on Gwendolen's wedding-night, Grandcourt's sudden death at sea. James avoids anything sensational. He may also have felt satisfied with the way such an episode suggests the lapse of time.

The problem here is not that the book covers six or seven years—shorter novels have successfully covered longer periods—but that the interest centres not so much on incidents as on processes, not on actions performed but on facts and conditions gradually understood, and it is difficult to represent these dramatically. The subject here is a marriage gone wrong—not, like Gwendolen's, one that's wrong from the start—and this is something that happens gradually. James has to find some substitute for the 'twenty "incidents"' which, starting from the day after the wedding, might have represented this process at impossible length. His solution is to leave a great gap of two and a half years, then to reapproach Isabel and Osmond obliquely, with a lot of new plot (Edward Rosier's suit for Pansy, Lord Warburton's return and the interest he takes in the girl—developments which, by showing us Pansy as marriageable, suggest time passed and a new generation come of age), so that sixty pages elapse between the end of the gap and Isabel's great vigil in Chapter 42. In the course of these sixty pages there are numerous hints that all is not well, and Chapter 42 comes as a clarification for us of what we have surmised as well as for Isabel of what she has lived through. Above all, the truth about her marriage becomes her thoughts on a particular occasion, and what sets them off—her coming in to find her husband and Madame Merle in close colloquy, she standing and he seated, 'unconsciously and familiarly associated'—is as 'mild' and ordinary as it is adequate, and produces, in the words of the preface, 'the maximum of intensity with the minimum of strain'.

At the end of her vigil her thoughts turn to her cousin Ralph, who now seems the very antithesis of her husband's baseness. Ralph's interest in Isbael, like Mr. Knightley's in Emma, has been the one right one from the start, but he is too young to have Mr. Knightley's august authority, besides which it is doubtful whether any character in James's uncertain world could credibly be so consistently in the right. Ralph's one decisive act, persuading his father to make Isabel rich, is that of a faith which we are at liberty to see as grounded in a romantic and deluded idealism, or simply as the extravagant homage of a man in love. Ralph is powerless to save Isabel: by making him a chronic invalid, James has made it impossible for him to play Mr. Knightley's part—to solve all her problems and consummate her happiness by making her his 'wife. His only prospect is death, deferred by the lively interest of watching her progress, and their only shared happiness, at his deathbed in Gardencourt, is in sharing 'the only knowledge that was not pure anguish—the knowledge that they were looking at the truth together'; the truth being that Osmond wouldn't have married her if she had been poor.

Ralph is close to the author in his role of loving observer who sees most. He does justice to the aesthetic attitude:

> Ralph had something of this same quality, this appearance of thinking that life was a matter of connoisseurship; but in Ralph it was an anomaly, a kind of humorous excrescence, whereas in Mr. Osmond it was the keynote. Ch. 24, p. 262

He cannot pretend to make his own life beautiful, so connoisseurship is 'a humorous excrescence', the sense of humour being a weapon of survival: if he took himself too seriously he would long ago have succumbed to despair. After an initial misunderstanding which exhibits the mixture of manners in James's best comic style (Ch. 10), Ralph also does justice to Henrietta, thus striking a precarious and merely personal balance between those Americans who reject European values and those whom those values corrupt. The sense of humour which makes him such an attractive character to the reader is fully appreciated only by Lord Warburton, which suggests that James saw it as a peculiarly English grace.

The other characters who surround the heroine sometimes suffer from James's need that they shall crop up in the right place at the right time to play their part in her 'ado'. Caspar Goodwood, who is supposed to be the manager of a cotton factory, has the leisure repeatedly to cross the Atlantic to make another appeal to the girl he loves. On one trip he spends two months in Paris considering whether or not he should proceed to Rome where Isabel is now living. It is doubtful whether such availability, such a ruthless and constant passion, and so much scrupulous hesitation are a credible combination in a busy 'mover of men'. Nevertheless, he is thoroughly real once he gets to grips with Isabel in one of their stormy scenes.

A more serious weakness is Lord Warburton, the only major character who is not an American. James had already done some good comic Englishmen in short stories, and he would soon be writing stories and a novel, *The Princess Casamassima* (1886), with a wholly English setting, but perhaps he wasn't yet ready to do an Englishman seriously. He makes Lord Warburton amusing to make him vivid, and makes Ralph amusing at his expense ('He says I don't understand my time. I understand it certainly better than he, who can neither abolish himself as a nuisance nor maintain himself as an institution.'), and this together with his supposed radicalism, of which we hear a good deal and see nothing, has the makings of a good comic character. Comedy invades the scene of his proposal to Isabel:

'There's one thing more,' he went on. 'You know, if you don't like Lockleigh—if you think it's damp or anything of that sort—you need never go within fifty miles of it. It's not damp, by the way; I've had the house thoroughly examined; it's perfectly safe and right. But if you shouldn't fancy it you needn't dream of living in it. There's no difficulty whatever about that; there are plenty of houses. I thought I'd just mention it; some people don't like a moat, you know. Good-bye.'   Ch. 12, p. 110

This is fine, but at the same time we're asked to believe that his feeling is deep enough to leave him unconsoled for several years —and thus available to complicate the plot towards the end— and that he makes a deep and serious appeal to Isabel. We can see why he won't do for Isabel, but we can't really see *him*, as a whole, though his parts are vivid.

The other characters are good enough, and some of them— Mrs. Touchett, the Countess Gemini—are brilliant. James hardly ever fails with a female character. However, they deserve to be appraised rather as a gallery of portraits, complementing and contrasting with one another and with Isabel. James began with her, not with them. He spoke of them later, in his preface, as

the definite array of contributions to Isabel Archer's history . . . It was as if they had simply, by an impulse of their own, floated into my ken, and all in response to my primary question: 'Well, what will she *do?*'

Quotations have been taken mostly from the first half of the novel, which contains the main expositions of character and theme. Concerned chiefly with whom and what the book is about, they have given no indication of how it improves as it goes along. Many novels decline towards the end as the author struggles to resolve a complicated plot. James's plot is not complicated and he has no elaborate resolution in view. The shadows close round Isabel and Ralph, and various minor characters, unable to do anything for the former, are charmingly attentive to the latter and to one another. James makes their kindness and warmth very real to us, placing a poignant emphasis on Isabel's isolation. Then, in forty pages (Chapters 49–52), comes a series of great clarifying scenes: Isabel with Madame Merle ('What have you to do with me?' ... 'Everything!'); Madame Merle with Osmond ('You've not only dried up my tears; you've dried up my soul ... You have made me as bad as yourself ... Have I been so vile all for nothing?'); Isabel with Osmond ('I must go to England' ... 'I shall not like it if you do.' 'Why should I mind that? You won't like it if I don't. You like nothing I do or don't do. You pretend to think I lie.'); Isabel with the Countess Gemini, who reveals Pansy's true parentage; Isabel with Pansy at the convent ('Oh, I'll do everything they want. Only if you're here I shall do it more easily.' ... 'I won't desert you.'); Isabel with Madame Merle ('I think I should like never to see you again.'). Then comes action for Isabel: the decisive journey to England to be with Ralph, and the decisive return.

James anticipated criticism of his ending:

> The obvious criticism of course will be that it is not finished—that I have not seen the heroine to the end of her situation—that I have left her *en l'air.*—This is both true and false. The *whole* of anything is never told; you can only take what groups together. What I have done has that unity—it groups together. NOTEBOOKS, p. 18

That is a good answer, and if you think of the sentimentality that afflicts the ending of even some of the finest Victorian novels, you'll hardly want to quarrel with the way James follows the death of Ralph with Caspar Goodwood's last passionate appeal and rejection, and follows that with the 'cheap comfort' of Henrietta's incorrigible optimism: 'Look here, Mr. Goodwood, just you wait!' Waiting is certainly what faces Isabel. Henrietta has advised her to leave Osmond 'before the worst comes ... before your character gets spoiled', but in her tragic pride Isabel clings to her ideal of freedom, though she's left with only the responsibility of an act freely performed, a burden freely shouldered:

> 'One must accept one's deeds. I married him before all the world; I was perfectly free; it was impossible to do anything more deliberate. One can't change that way.' Ch. 47, p. 488

Besides, she has promised not to desert Pansy. She will continue to worry about her duty, and clearly she is not going to throw herself under a train. 'Deep inside her—deeper than any appetite for renunciation—was the sense that life would be her business for a long time to come.'

The Portrait of a Lady is a remarkable novel. For its length it is singularly concentrated and coherent. With its economy of incident and its placing of the centre of interest more than ever before in the consciousness of the protagonist, it looks forward to the future development of the novel, both within James's work and beyond it. It gives serious treatment to an unsuccessful marriage, which in fiction had traditionally been a subject for comedy. It brings evil and the spectre of tragedy into the drawing-rooms of modern Europe, without closing the door to social comedy. It has a special place in the long series of 19th-century novels in which the social position of women and their efforts to emancipate themselves are a prominent issue. It raises this issue to its most sophisticated level and describes a very deliberate attempt, by applying the highest moral and aesthetic standards, to find what might be called an aristocratic solution to the problem. In so doing, it goes beyond the relatively narrow terms of the debate as a fact of social history and makes a profound literary statement about the relations of art and morality, and about the liberty of the individual. Two brief quotations sum up the ideals in question:

> For the moment, Isabel went to the Hôtel de Paris as often as she thought well; the measure of propriety was in the canon of taste, and there couldn't have been a better proof that morality was, so to speak, a matter of earnest appreciation.   Ch. 45, p. 463

> Her notion of the aristocratic life was simply the union of great knowledge with great liberty; the knowledge would give one a sense of duty and the liberty a sense of enjoyment.
>
>   Ch. 42, p. 431

James himself says nothing to discredit them.

5

The Bostonians (1886)

Apart from *The Ivory Tower*, which remained unfinished at his death, *The Bostonians* is the only long novel by James set wholly in America and among Americans. He had been living in Europe for nearly ten years when he began it, and although he was to return to America for short periods, by now he regarded England as his home. He had lived in New York and Boston, where the novel is largely set, for much of his boyhood and youth and he knew them well, but he had found American society increasingly jejune and the American scene increasingly unattractive, so it is not surprising that the novel gives a satirical picture of some aspects of American urban life. No one except the thoroughly discreditable Mrs. Luna ever expresses anything like a 'European' point of view, but James projects his criticism through two principal characters. One is the hero Basil Ransom, a Southerner from Mississippi who has fought against the Federal forces in the Civil War (1861–4), and views with scepticism the life of the Northern cities to which he has come to repair his broken fortunes. The other, his Bostonian cousin Olive Chancellor, combines the disgust of a refined sensibility at modern vulgarity with the professional discontent of the reformer. So James has his detached and critical observers and through them he can dramatise that debate about civilisation and the social conditions that promote or degrade it which is a perennial feature of his work. No English-born novelist had yet done anything as explicit as this for English society in the 19th century.

The particular issues on which the debate centres in *The*

Bostonians were already singled out by James in a notebook entry of 1883:

> I wished to write a very American tale, a tale very characteristic of our social conditions, and I asked myself what was the most salient and peculiar point in our social life. The answer was: the situation of women, the decline of the sentiment of sex, the agitation on their behalf.   NOTEBOOKS, p. 47

'The situation of women' is a latent issue in many 19th-century novels. Not only the poor were deprived. Condemned to a largely ornamental role at home and in society, not granted even the freedom of the club and the smoking room, and hardly allowed the management of their own children, the wives of the idle rich had their frustrations too.

An instance of the supposedly emancipated woman can be found in the ludicrous figure of Kukshina in Turgenev's *Fathers and Sons* (1862), but James's novel is, as far as I know, the first to show the traditional role of women in society being explicitly and seriously challenged. This challenge was of course a fact of American social history, not an invention of James's. His contribution to the debate is to have treated the movement for reform in a satirical manner. Not only does he show it to be a prey to the vulgarities of modern publicity and the exploitation of mercenary interests: its most idealistic and high-minded representatives are chronically muddled and unpractical, ridden by a vague and sentimental rhetoric, and the plot of the novel is so arranged that the happy resolution of its central conflict involves the complete discomfiture of the reformers.

The Bostonians is perhaps his most polemical work. It is full of general ideas, and one difference between characters and ideas is that the former have a particular life and the latter a general one: they live or have lived in the real world outside the novel, as well as within it, and the reader may well be acquainted with them and have his own opinions about them before he sits down to read it. This raises some more or less theoretical questions. Can the reader enjoy or approve of a book that seems to endorse ideas contrary to his own? Do general ideas in a work of art demand to be either accepted or rejected as they do in real life? Or are they merely one motive force, among many, in the lives of the characters? Does the novel cease to be a work of art and begin to resemble a pamphlet or a tract in so far as the author seems to take sides himself?

In *The Bostonians*, in any case, the ideas about women's rights are so well embodied in the particular situation the novel presents, that it is perfectly possible to share the hero's critical view of them while we read, without regarding the movement for the emancipation of women as a bad thing. On the other hand it would be wrong to explain away Basil Ransom's views as merely the product of his Southern background, temperament or ambitions. A passage like the following is not just a piece of characterisation:

> 'I am so far from thinking, as you set forth the other night, that there is not enough woman in our general life, that it has long been pressed home to me that there is a good deal too much. The whole generation is womanized; the masculine tone is passing out of the world; it's a feminine, a nervous, hysterical, chattering, canting age, an age of hollow phrases and false delicacy and exaggerated solicitudes and coddled sensibilities, which, if we don't soon look out, will usher in the reign of mediocrity, of the feeblest and flattest and the most pretentious that has ever been. The masculine character, the ability to dare and endure, to know and yet not fear reality, to look the world in the face and take it for what it is— a very queer and partly very base mixture—that is what I want to preserve, or rather, as I may say, to recover; and I must tell you that I don't in the least care what becomes of you ladies while I make the attempt.'   Ch. 34, p. 290

Ransom's views, 'the rejection of which by leading periodicals was certainly not a matter for surprise', are not just the lumber of a past age. *The Bostonians* could affect our view of our own age. Whether it does so or not, James shows how general ideas tend always to be compromised by the other considerations that belong to a particular situation, and we are reminded that particular situations are, after all, the only soil in which those ideas can grow and prove themselves.

The relation between the two Bostonians who champion the cause of feminism was described by James in his notebook as an 'intimate friendship . . . one of those friendships between women which are so common in New England'. A little less than half the book depicts the consolidation of this friendship, and the rest its undermining. Olive Chancellor, rich and refined, 'unmarried by every implication of her being' and already an ardent reformer, develops a passionate interest in a beautiful girl whose parents live on the disreputable fringe of reformist circles and have already discovered in their daughter a gift for public speaking which they are eager to exploit. She virtually bribes the parents to let the girl come and live with her so that they may work together in the cause of women's emancipation. Olive's wealth makes it unnecessary for Verena to produce her eloquence on poor occasions, and enables her to keep the girl to herself with the jealous possessiveness of the lover that she is. James chronicles marvellously the gradual subjection of the one young woman to the other. The same radical differences in their natures and backgrounds that make the subjection possible prevent Verena from returning Olive's devotion in full measure, and prepare the catastrophe. Their different responses to each other are a source of comedy before they become one of tragedy:

> Verena wondered afterward why she had not been more afraid of her—why, indeed, she had not turned and saved herself by darting out of the room. But it was not in this young woman's nature to be either timid or cautious; she had yet to make acquaintance with the sentiment of fear. She knew too little of the world to have learned to mistrust sudden enthusiasms, and if she had had a suspicion it would have been (in accordance with common worldly knowledge) the wrong one—the suspicion that such a whimsical liking would burn itself out. She could not have that one, for there was a light in Miss Chancellor's magnified face which seemed to say that a sentiment, with her, might consume its object, might consume Miss Chancellor, but would never consume itself. Verena, as yet, had no sense

of being scorched; she was only agreeably warmed. She also had dreamed of a friendship, though it was not what she had dreamed of most, and it came over her that this was the one which fortune might have been keeping. She never held back.

'Do you live here all alone?' she asked of Olive.

'I shouldn't if you would come and live with me!'

Even this really passionate rejoinder failed to make Verena shrink; she thought it so possible that in the wealthy class people made each other such easy proposals. It was a part of the romance, the luxury, of wealth; it belonged to the world of invitations, in which she had had so little share. But it seemed almost a mockery when she thought of the little house in Cambridge, where the boards were loose in the steps of the porch.   Ch. 11, p. 72

On the one hand the language of passion ('burn', 'consume', 'scorch'); on the other the comedy of misunderstanding and social uncertainty which gives the measure of Verena's cool and wondering acquiescence.

The personal incongruity of the two women is complicated by the dubious connection between the personal and the public motives of their cohabitation. Olive is devoted to the cause of women, eager for battle and not indifferent to the limelight of a public crusade, so Verena's gift is a wonderful opportunity for her to enter the public arena in a way that, with her 'fits of tragic shyness', she never could have on her own. Yet she wants Verena all to herself, and every public exposure is a threat to her possession. We can rejoice in her successful struggles with Verena's parents, with Matthias Pardon the journalist and with the Burrages, because we share her disgust at their various corruptions. By turns we admire her refinement, smile at the efforts of her honesty to reconcile selfish and altruistic motives, and find her extremely unattractive, not least because she has no sense of humour. This last failing marks her lack of objectivity and sharply distinguishes her way of seeing things from the generally ironical tone of the narrative. These checks on our sympathy allow us to desire that Verena shall be freed from Olive's grasp and rescued from the celibate state which it is only too clear that Nature has not made her for. Yet the pain is great, and in suffering it Olive rises to something like a tragic stature. When she wanders on the lonely shore of the Cape, faced with Verena's final betrayal of her love and ambitions, so long foreseen and so arduously prevented, the epithet seems justified. Verena sees it too:

> She had a vision of those dreadful years; she knew that Olive would never get over the disappointment. It would touch her in the point where she felt everything most keenly; she would be incurably lonely and eternally humiliated. Ch. 38, p. 334

Verena blames herself, but we see that in so far as character is fate, this was Olive's destiny. This is a psychological matter, thoroughly explained and illustrated in the earlier part of the book. As Ransom sees, Olive is 'morbid', one of those people who 'take things hard'; 'no one could help her: that was what made her tragic'. Nowadays we should probably use an ugly word like 'maladjusted', even 'chronically' so: 'It was the usual things of life that filled her with silent rage; which was natural enough, inasmuch as, to her vision, almost everything that was usual was iniquitous.' James doesn't offer any scientific explanation of her condition, but he embodies it unforgettably in her behaviour. What makes her case not just peculiar but exemplary, giving her 'something of the ecstasy of the martyr', is the spirit with which she fights her disability. The battle is comic or tragic according to what is at stake, but her last passionate struggle for possession of the loved one has the intensity of Racine; it would not be absurd to compare her to Hermione, Roxane or Phèdre. But James has hit upon the very plausible connection between revolutionary ardour and psychological maladjustment. Medieval science would class her as melancholic or 'atrabilious'. Of course not all revolutionaries suffer from a preponderance of black bile, and by endowing his reformist heroine with such a temperament, James has weighted the scales against her as heavily as Molière did against Le Misanthrope, who is just as possessive as Olive towards his beloved.

Basil Ransom, the hero of the novel, is the opposite of Olive Chancellor not only in sex but in temperament ('He himself, by nature, took things easy'; 'privacy for Basil Ransom consisted entirely in what he called "laying-off"'), in background (a Mississippian, he fought on the Southern side in the Civil War; Olive Chancellor's two brothers died for the Northern cause), and in opinions. The differences in their morality and outlook are as fundamental as any between Americans and Europeans in James's 'international' works. In the conflict between them James is too good an artist to take sides in a spirit of dogmatism. His job is to make us understand both points of view.

Our siding with Ransom against Olive Chancellor is not determined by the general rightness or wrongness of their views, in James's or our opinion. We side with Ransom firstly because, in the opening chapters which bring the two characters together, we see more from his point of view than from hers. His view is the dominant one for the first eighty pages. At Miss Birdseye's (Chapters 4–9) his observations are assimilated to the narrator's; they have a similar tone of amused and ironical detachment. Olive's thoughts and feelings, on the other hand, are quite distinct and given in a special style, *her* style reported indirectly, which 'places' them for the reader (for example, the last paragraph of Chapter 5). Her view is more subjective than his—partly because more charged and distorted by emotion—but we see it more objectively. It's true that James occasionally makes a show of dissociating himself from Ransom's view ('Poor Ransom announced this fact to himself as if he had made a great discovery, but in reality he had never been so "Bœotian" as at that moment . . . it must be repeated that he was very provincial'), but this is soon dropped. The following passage shows how his view is assimilated to the narrator's:

'The use of a truly amiable woman is to make some honest man happy,' Ransom said, with a sententiousness of which he was perfectly aware.

It was so marked that it caused her to stop short in the middle of the broad walk, while she looked at him with shining eyes. 'See here, Mr. Ransom, do you know what strikes me?' she exclaimed. 'The interest you take in me isn't really controversial—a bit. It's quite personal!' She was the most extraordinary girl; she could speak such words as those without the smallest look of added

> consciousness coming into her face, without the least supposable
> intention of coquetry, or any visible purpose of challenging the
> young man to say more.   Ch. 25, p. 207

The last sentence could be either Ransom's thought or the
narrator's comment, and we are not even likely to notice the
ambiguity. On further inspection, you could say that the first
clause is Ransom's delighted exclamation to himself, made
indirect only by the tense; that the sentence goes on to voice his
thoughts in the narrator's words; and that in the last clause we
are back with the narrator—but couldn't it just as well have
ended '... or any visible purpose of challenging *you* to say
more.'?

The passage shows us Ransom enjoying Verena as we do, for
what she is. Olive's love, on the other hand, is repressive. This is
a second reason why we must side with Ransom: we want him
to rescue her from a life that is wrong for her and threatens to
become a prison. This rescue operation would have been a
relatively crude affair if Verena had been as conscious of her
prison as most distressed heroines are. As it is, the interest of the
struggle is psychological, centring on Verena's gradual awakening to her nature and destiny.

Thirdly, whatever we may think of Ransom's ideas in the
abstract, they work in practice: he can live with them without
hypocrisy. In Olive's case, on the other hand, there is no *necessary*
connection, in fact there is a yawning discrepancy, between her
principles and her emotional needs. Publicly she wants to free all
women from the masculine tyranny, but privately she wants to
bind one woman to herself as exclusively as any husband would.
This discrepancy drives her to do what she has scorned others for
doing more blatantly: to use her idealism for selfish ends, as
when 'Olive's most passionate protest was summed up in her
saying that if Verena were to forsake them it would put back the
emancipation of women a hundred years'. Ransom is never
driven to such dishonest expedients.

The book is really the story of two rescues: first Olive rescues
Verena from her parents and other exploiters, then Ransom

rescues her from Olive. James intertwines the two operations very neatly. Ransom comes forcefully into the field on the day after Verena's lecture at the Burrages' house in New York, just at the moment when Olive, who has hitherto held off the Burrages rather successfully, is sorely tempted to compromise with them and enter into partnership with Mrs. Burrage in the management of Verena as the wife of the docile young Henry Burrage. She is tempted because she knows Ransom is in the field, and the Burrages seem very much the lesser of two evils. However, Ransom makes so much progress with Verena during the very hours when Olive is cloistered with Mrs. Burrage, that the two Bostonians immediately take flight for their native city, which puts the Burrages out of the picture for good. This is a fine bit of plotting on James's part, worthy of the successful playwright that he never managed to be, and it brings the central section of the novel (Chapters 21–34) to a dramatic climax.

Successful rescues are the stuff of comedy, and there is the additional happy fact that Verena is as yet unharmed by the mainly odious people she is rescued from. To have made this credible, in fact to have made her so charming without her detesting all those odious people, is quite an achievement. She is a thoroughly genial creature, a 'brilliantly healthy nature' like Felix Young in *The Europeans*. James speaks of the 'supreme success simply to have been made as she was made', and of how 'she had kept the consummate innocence of the American girl, that innocence which was the greatest of all, for it had survived the abolition of walls and locks'. But she is not at all simple-minded: she bears her burden of intelligence and proves, to use James's phrase, a worthy 'vessel of consciousness'.

The real odiousness, which has miraculously failed to contaminate Verena, but against which the full sharpness of James's satire is directed, does not consist in any ideas about the rights of women, though that movement is seen to suffer from it, but in the larger fact of modern 'publicity', the invasion of private life by the public interest, and the consequent abuse of language and vulgarisation of manners. This invasion is as insidious in a democratic society where it is made by the mass media (in

James's day just the newspapers), by advertising and by the lifting of so-called 'taboos' about sex and other private matters, as in a totalitarian society where it is made with a franker brutality by the secret police. *The Bostonians* was perhaps the first great novel to expose a tendency that has gone a good deal further in our time. James can treat it pretty lightly:

> About the middle of December, Miss Chancellor received a visit from Matthias Pardon, who had come to ask her what she meant to do about Verena. She had never invited him to call upon her, and the appearance of a gentleman whose desire to see her was so irrepressible as to dispense with such a preliminary was not in her career an accident frequent enough to have taught her equanimity. She thought Mr. Pardon's visit a liberty; but, if she expected to convey this idea to him by withholding any suggestion that he should sit down, she was greatly mistaken, inasmuch as he cut the ground from under her feet by himself offering her a chair. His manner represented hospitality enough for both of them, and she was obliged to listen, on the edge of her sofa (she could at least seat herself where she liked), to his extraordinary inquiry.
>
> Ch. 17, p. 122

This particular matter of the newspapers is the subject of other works, notably *The Reverberator* (1888), an excellent short novel, and the two tales 'John Delavoy' (1898) and 'The Papers' (1903). *A propos* of *The Reverberator* he wrote in his notebook:

> One sketches one's age but imperfectly if one doesn't touch on that particular matter: the invasion, the impudence and shamelessness, of the newspaper and the interviewer, the devouring *publicity* of life, the extinction of all sense between public and private. It is the highest expression of the note of 'familiarity', the sinking of *manners*, in so many ways, which the democratisation of the world brings with it.
>
> p. 82

In 'The Papers,' a very fine late story, the hero and heroine are themselves journalists, and engaged to be married. The young man is so luridly successful at his job that the girl is eventually appalled and forces him, as Ransom forces Verena, to quit the public arena by giving up his profession. An invasion of privacy not by a journalist but by a literary scholar is the subject of 'The Aspern Papers' (see Chapter 7).

As for the abuse of language, this is a perennial subject of sophisticated literature, especially of satire. One form of abuse that the satirist can expose is the way people use language to disguise their real motives when these are too base to be frankly admitted. (Thus in *The Merchant's Tale* the exalted language of courtly love is incongruously and inconsistently used to describe the processes of lust; and in Swift's 'Modest Proposal' the tones of an innocently practical man of business highlight a nation's callous indifference to the plight of a subject people.) There is plenty of baseness to be concealed by James's characters. Verena's father, for example, longs for publicity, sees his daughter's gift as his best hope of achieving it, and covers up his low desires in habitually high-flown language. Here we see him in action in a brilliant passage of direct narration alternating with indirect speech:

> He was solemnly civil to Miss Chancellor, handed her the dishes at table over and over again, and ventured to intimate that the apple-fritters were very fine; but, save for this, alluded to nothing more trivial than the regeneration of humanity and the strong hope he felt that Miss Birdseye would again have one of her delightful gatherings. With regard to this latter point he explained that it was not in order that he might again present his daughter to the company, but simply because on such occasions there was a valuable interchange of hopeful thought, a contact of mind with mind. If Verena had anything suggestive to contribute to the social problem, the opportunity would come—that was part of their faith. They couldn't reach out for it and try and push their way; if they were wanted, their hour would strike; if they were not, they would just keep still and let others press forward who seemed to be called. If they were called they would know it; and if they weren't, they could just hold on to each other as they had always done. Tarrant was very fond of alternatives, and he mentioned several others; it was never his fault if his listeners failed to think him impartial. They hadn't much, as Miss Chancellor could see; she could tell by their manner of life that they hadn't raked in the dollars; but they had faith that, whether one raised one's voice or simply worked on

in silence, the principal difficulties would straighten themselves out; and they had also a considerable experience of great questions. Tarrant spoke as if, as a family, they were prepared to take charge of them on moderate terms.
Ch. 15, p. 99

He uses a nauseating mixture of religious language ('faith', being 'called', 'raising one's voice'), the vaguely high-flown ('a valuable interchange of hopeful thought', 'the principal difficulties', 'their hour would strike'), and the humble colloquial ('they couldn't reach out for it and try and push their way', 'they could just hold on to each other as they had always done', 'they hadn't raked in the dollars'). These elements combine to give a tell-tale uncertainty of style, a blurring of linguistic distinctions, to the way he expresses the flatulent vagueness of his thought. The *intended* effect is to suggest a humble but discerning patience which is the very opposite of the truth. The narrator's comments in the last and ante-penultimate sentences are the more effective for their oblique discretion. They don't seriously interrupt the flow, or make the reader feel that the author is breathing down his neck. They are not clearly Olive's reflections, but they *could* be hers.

The minor characters are mostly odious or ludicrous or both, and for all of them James finds a characteristic language. He makes extensive use of indirect speech, and this half-submerging of their utterance emphasises its peculiarities. (The speech of Matthias Pardon, the journalist, is rendered almost entirely in a reported form (Chapters 16–17), which is indeed a kind of justice for a reporter.) They have more individual life, more idiosyncrasy than is often the case in James, and something of the free memorability of the best minor characters in Dickens. But James should be praised for avoiding that mechanical crudity of caricature into which Dickens sometimes falls—compare the discreet use James makes of Selah Tarrant's 'big, even, carnivorous teeth' with the way Dickens mechanically and tiresomely repeats his references to the dental equipment of another unsatisfied character, Mr. Carker of *Dombey and Son*. He should also be praised for his structural economy: he makes all his minor characters relevant to his main themes, to the subject of the book, in one way or another, and he skilfully integrates them into the plot. The use of Miss Birdseye and Doctor Prance is especially notable in this last respect, in Chapters 23, 35-6 and 38-9.

The minor female characters can be seen as a series of pertinent comments on James's stated theme: 'the situation of women, the decline of the sentiment of sex, the agitation on their behalf'. There is Miss Birdseye 'with her universal familiarity', the ancient and selfless champion of the oppressed, her vagueness genuinely rosy in contrast to Selah Tarrant's spurious rouge. Like Doctor Prance, who 'was incapable of asking him a personal question', she is both a woman and no woman:

> There was a legend that an Hungarian had once possessed himself of her affections, and had disappeared after robbing her of everything she possessed. This, however, was very apocryphal, for she had never possessed anything, and it was open to grave doubt that she could have entertained a sentiment so personal. She was in love, even in those days, only with causes, and she languished only for emancipations. Ch. 4, p. 26

But whereas Miss Birdseye is all softness, 'muffled in laxity', Doctor Prance is 'tough and technical'. She is also a genuinely emancipated female whose quiet devotion to her profession is an implicit derogatory comment on the vague aspirations of the reformers. In both these characters the ludicrous and the likeable are splendidly combined, and the combination is much appreciated by Ransom. Behind them, and behind Mrs. Farrinder, whose introduction in Chapter 4 is a great descriptive set-piece, we glimpse 'the serious, tired people, in their bonnets and overcoats', sitting patiently in bare, gas-lit rooms, but ready, when roused, 'to glow like a company of heroes'.

On the other side, that of the 'unconverted', the women are not ludicrous so much as corrupt. Olive's sister Mrs. Luna, a much degraded version of the Baroness in *The Europeans*, is sexually ostentatious and, behind the forms of Europeanised manners, as vulgar as anyone in the book. Apart from her function in the plot, as a link between Olive and Basil Ransom, she provides a contrast to her sister's refinement and opinions—

almost a motive for the latter—and, with her money and conservative views, a temptation for Ransom. Actually, there is a gulf between her 'soft' conservatism and Ransom's 'hard' variety, and it is one of the small felicities of this partly political novel to have marked a distinction here (see especially the end of Chapter 21) which is constantly overlooked in real life, both by 'soft' conservatives and by socialists, though no doubt for different motives, and which now confuses the modern issue of conservation.

Finally there is Mrs. Burrage, a truly masterful woman, who together with her son constitutes the most serious temptation for Olive. Henry Burrage, says his mother, is 'an angel', which is her way of saying that if Olive lets him marry Verena he'll be as submissive to his wife as he is to his mother. According to Olive's assessment, he is 'as much in love as the feebler passions of the age permitted'—one of those nice touches which show that in one respect at least, Olive is Basil Ransom's cousin spiritually as well as by consanguinity: they are both moral aristocrats. But however weak his passion, Henry Burrage's suit is formidably reinforced by the various amenities—financial, social, aesthetic—which the wealthy Burrage family can offer a poor girl with a large appetite for life. This is a recurrent subject in James's work: how questions of love and marriage in a sophisticated society are complicated and confused, sometimes disastrously, by the attractions of aesthetic refinement, social position and material ease.

In a brilliant scene in Chapter 32 Mrs. Burrage, speaking for her son, makes her appeal to Olive, whose influence on Verena, *almost* rightly, she measures by her own on her 'poor boy'. The cruder advantages she offers, of money and social influence—'all New York shall sit at her feet'—are given their full weight, and Mrs. Burrage simulates, with proper moderation, an enthusiasm for the great female cause. Olive is not impervious to these attractions. But with the cunning of her own corruption Mrs. Burrage works most effectively of all on Olive's personal attachment to Verena and fear of losing her. With a frankness that approaches brutality, she refers to Verena as 'the very person in the world you want most to keep unmarried', and hits uncannily on the very possibility Olive most dreads, namely that if Verena doesn't marry Henry Burrage, there are much less amenable men about, to whom she might fall prey: 'I don't mean anyone in particular; but, for instance, there is the young man to whom she asked me to send an invitation to my party, and who looked to me like a possible admirer.' This is just a shot in the dark, but it hits the mark. Olive knows she is referring to Basil Ransom and has already sensed how dangerous he is. What she doesn't know, because Verena has concealed it from her, is how Ransom managed to get an invitation. Mrs. Luna has already suggested to her that Verena asked for it to be sent, but Olive knew she was being malicious and indignantly rejected an idea that had such painful implications. Now she learns the truth of it from Mrs. Burrage, who doesn't know it's news to her, but couldn't have used the knowledge to more cruel effect if she *had* known. This complicated piece of dramatic irony is not the only one in the book.

Where else in literature do we find such exuberant and good-humoured comedy made out of the corrupt, the mean and the absurd? In Ben Jonson, perhaps, or in Gogol. A comparison with Gogol's novel *Dead Souls* (1842), though unpromising in many ways, has some further ground in the rich particularity of the physical background in both novels. Density of specification in this respect is not something James is often credited with; indeed it is a common complaint against some of his work that he gives too little of it to support such large structures. This charge may have some justice against *The Awkward Age*, *The Golden Bowl* or even *The Princess Casamassima*, but it would be absurd to bring it against *The Bostonians*:

> And then Mrs. Luna, sitting with her sister, much withdrawn, in one of the windows of the big, hot, faded parlour of the boarding-house in Tenth Street, where there was a rug before the chimney representing a Newfoundland dog saving a child from drowning, and a row of chromo-lithographs on the walls, imparted to her the impression she had received the evening before—the impression of Basil Ransom's keen curiosity about Verena Tarrant.
>
> Ch. 29, p. 242

The description of the rug is a thoroughly gratuitous detail, but we couldn't wish it away. James is not often as 'irresponsible' as this—a matter of regret to some readers, perhaps—though he does say disarmingly of the fine description of the Dutch grocery next to Ransom's lodgings in New York (Ch. 21):

> I mention it not on account of any particular influence it may have had on the life or the thoughts of Basil Ransom, but for old acquaintance sake and that of local colour; besides which, a figure is nothing without a setting, and our young man came and went every day, with rather an indifferent, unperceiving step, it is true, among the objects I have briefly designated.

That remark about figures without settings, after his previous admission, is slightly tongue-in-cheek. James was a great admirer of Balzac, but he could never have subscribed to Balzac's rather dogmatic views on the interdependence of character and environment ('*Toute sa personne explique la pension, comme la pension implique sa personne,*' as Balzac said of Madame Vauquer in *Le Père Goriot*). James takes a higher view of man's moral liberty and his independence of the physical conditions in which he lives. Nevertheless, *The Bostonians* is full of extremely specific and convincing details of physical background: the view across the Charles from Olive's drawing-room, with 'the desolate suburban horizons, peeled and made bald by the rigour of the season'; the vestibules of the big Boston hotels, 'the piled-up luggage, the convenient spittoons, the elbowing loungers, the disconsolate "guests", the truculent Irish porters, the rows of shaggy-backed men in strange hats, writing letters at a table inlaid with advertisements'; Central Park in New York, where 'groups of the unemployed, the children of disappointment from beyond the seas, propped themselves against the low, sunny wall . . . and on the other side the commercial vista of the Sixth Avenue stretched away with a remarkable absence of aerial perspective'; the new suburban houses at Cambridge which 'stood, for the most part, on small eminences, lifted above the impertinence of hedge or paling, well up before the world'; and Cape Cod in August, when 'the ripeness of summer lay upon the land, and yet there was nothing in the country Basil

Ransom traversed that seemed susceptible of maturity; nothing but the apples in the little tough, dense orchards, which gave a suggestion of sour fruition here and there, and the tall, bright golden-rod at the bottom of the bare stone dykes'.

James had known all these places in his boyhood, and in the assurance with which he re-creates them there is a mixture of affection and detachment—the affection elicited by youthful memories, and the detachment of a man who had found that Europe offered richer satisfactions than his native land to 'the painter's eye'. The affection comes out most strongly in the scenes at Marmion (Cape Cod), not far from Newport where he spent some of the happiest years of his boyhood:

> There were lights now in the windows of some of the houses, and Doctor Prance mentioned to her companion several of the inhabitants of the little town, who appeared all to rejoice in the prefix of captain. They were retired shipmasters; there was quite a little nest of these worthies, two or three of whom might be seen lingering in their dim doorways, as if they were conscious of a want of encouragement to sit up, and yet remembered the nights in far-away waters when they would not have thought of turning in at all.
>
> Ch. 35, p. 304

Here imagination reaches out to include in the scene lives that are quite untouched by the story, as irrelevant as those of the two carriers in *Henry the Fourth, Part I* who tumble back on to the road discussing their horses' ailments and the lack of chamber-pots in the inn.

The change of scene from the city to Cape Cod for the critical struggle between Olive and Ransom leaves the satire largely behind. It separates the three principal characters from their usual background, together with Miss Birdseye and Doctor Prance, the only two minor characters who aren't odious. The natural setting is right for the bare, basic struggle in which, for Verena, natural forces are to get the better of habit and constraint:

> When she saw him a little way off, about five o'clock—the hour she usually went out to meet him—waiting for her at a bend

of the road which lost itself, after a winding, straggling mile or two, in the indented, insulated 'point', where the wandering bee droned through the hot hours with a vague, misguided flight, she felt that his tall, watching figure, with the low horizon behind, represented well the importance, the towering eminence he had in her mind—the fact that he was just now, to her vision, the most definite and upright, the most incomparable, object in the world. If he had not been at his post when she expected him she would have had to stop and lean against something, for weakness; her whole being would have throbbed more painfully than it throbbed at present, though finding him there made her nervous enough.

Ch. 38, p. 332

The contrasting images of vertical and horizontal, attention and wandering, definition and vagueness, give expression here to levels of feeling which James could never have dealt with more explicitly or analytically. There is no reason to regret that he expressed them poetically instead. His reticence in the treatment of sexual feeling is no greater than that of the society he was writing about. For them, physical sex was a specially private matter and not, in itself, a subject they had the vocabulary to discuss. Still, *The Bostonians* is about sex. It depicts a struggle in which the sexual power of the characters is latent but decisive; it is not a separable fact about them, but permeates their being, moral as well as physical. That James was able to suggest as much, is an effect of art. It is also realistic, for though our relations with others are sometimes specifically sexual and we may sometimes want to speak about them in a specifically sexual way, yet men are men and women are women all the time, and we recognise and acknowledge this as a moral and social as well as a physical fact about one another—or rather, our recognition of it varies from person to person, from age to age and from one society to another, and the strength and form of it are determining factors in the life of the individual and his society. 'The decline of the sentiment of sex': what do James's words mean? Not, surely, that the sexual power of urban Americans in the 1870s was less than it had been, but rather that the forms which that society provided for the expression of the sexual life of its members had become in some way inadequate, and that the quality of private life had thereby suffered, with consequent reverberations in the public sphere.

This was a profound critical insight. What does the novel show us of 'the possible other case, the case rich and edifying where the actuality is pretentious and vain'? I would instance the conversation, too long to quote, between Ransom and Verena at the end of Chapter 24, in which they renew their acquaintance after a gap of eighteen months. The dialogue is full of amusing superficial characterisation, and beneath its surface we see the ebb and flow of the girl's feeling, her tentative advances and withdrawals of confidence, the pull of impulse, the contrary pull of reflexion and moral judgment, her embarrassed reconciliation of the two, and Ransom's delighted appreciation of it all. The rapid but detailed notation of these complexities by the narrator enhances the gaiety of the passage. In the moving scene which follows, when they visit the Memorial Hall at Harvard, built to commemorate the lives of those who fell in the Civil War, one feels James is giving way to general American feelings, but these are beautifully blended with the private story. The lovers pass briefly into the shadow of history, of war and death, and acknowledge it without prejudice to the rightness of their happiness:

> He stood before her, tracing a figure on the mosaic pavement with his cane, conscious that in a moment they had become more intimate. They were discussing their affairs, which had nothing to do with the heroic symbols that surrounded them; but their affairs had suddenly grown so serious that there was no want of decency in their lingering there for the purpose. Ch. 25, p.211

For all its rich diversity, *The Bostonians* is not one of James's longest novels. It has a time-span of two and a half years, but the relation of the number of pages to the passing of time is extremely variable. Out of those two and a half years, four days, or rather four periods of twenty-four hours, occupy two hundred and thirty pages, that is to say three-fifths of the total number. One of these days comes at the beginning, two about the middle, and the fourth at the end. Thus there is a certain balance, as well as a striking contrast, between the very brief periods singled out for extensive representation, with a lot of dialogue, and the long periods between them which are treated in a more sketchy and indirect manner with a preponderance of narrative. In this way James is able to give much of the book the intense immediacy and the scenic quality of drama, while he compensates for the tendency of the more narrative sections to cool down and lose touch, by his narrative wit, by frequent narration from a particular character's point of view, and by a vivid use of indirect speech. The reader has the impression not only of a great diversity of scene and character, but of a tight structure and a pace variable but never slow, which quickens in the last thirty pages to a breath-taking climax.

Some contemporary critics took exception to the ending. One wrote: 'Mr. Henry James snuffs out the light of his story with a disagreeable sort of snap in his last sentence.' But surely the wry tone of that sentence is exactly right. Will Ransom be justified only if Verena never sheds another tear? Is a life without tears the only happiness?

The gaiety and pace of the narrative, the feeling for the scene, the satire of public life and the vulgarity of the modern democratic age, the moral aristocracy combined, in Ransom and Verena, with a large appetite for life and talent for happiness—all these qualities of *The Bostonians* recall more than anything else the work of Stendhal, who, oddly enough, was the only major French novelist of the 19th century James never wrote about.

6

What Maisie Knew (1897)

'Mamma doesn't care for me,' she said very simply. 'Not really.
Child as she was, her little long history was in the words.

Like *Washington Square*, sixteen years before, *What Maisie
Knew* began from the idea of a young girl deprived of her
parents' affection. Maisie, the 'luckless child of a divorced couple',
is more obviously a victim than Catherine Sloper, but in each
case James conceived a heroine at a marked psychological disadvantage, and instead of exploiting the possibilities for pathos and
sentimentality in this situation, he brings out in the young girl
qualities of intelligence and fortitude which enable her to get
the better of her disadvantages, and he gives his narrative a comic
surface that holds pathos and tragedy at bay. These effects are
more marked in the later novel: Maisie is younger but brighter
than Catherine; she is bandied about between one parent and
another in a way that would reduce most children to psychological wrecks, but preserves her good humour and makes the
best of every weird complication as it arises; James develops the
plot to produce effects of repetition and symmetry whose dramatic irony is highly entertaining; and he drives the story along at
a brisk pace, in a style that brilliantly gets round the limitation of
restricting his narrative to the heroine's point of view.

In 1892 James heard the story of a divorced couple to whom
the court, exceptionally, had assigned alternate custody of the
child: she was to go to and fro between them, 'rebounding from
racquet to racquet like a tennis ball or a shuttlecock'. In their
mutual hatred, each parent had at first sought to keep the child
jealously from the other. Then, one of them having remarried,

and wanting rid of it, James saw how the game might change to that of leaving the child as long as possible on the hands of the other parent. Starting from there, it occurred to him that 'for a proper symmetry the second parent should marry too . . . The misfortune of the little victim' would then become 'altogether exemplary'. In a later Notebook entry he refers to 'the child whose parents divorce and who makes such an extraordinary link between a succession of people'. He was beginning to work out what he called 'the ironic interest'. The irony is threefold: firstly, having been the victim of her parents' separation, Maisie becomes the means of bringing her step-parents together; secondly, though herself all innocence, she thus becomes 'a centre and pretext for a fresh system of misbehaviour', namely the step-parents' adultery: and thirdly, 'not less than the chance of misery and of a degraded state, the chance of happiness and of an improved state might be here involved for the child, round about whom the complexity of life would thus turn to fineness, to richness . . .' (Preface).

The plot was accordingly developed with a view to 'a proper symmetry'. Ida, Maisie's mother, engages a governess, Miss Overmore, who is young and pretty and is soon seduced and married by Beale Farange, Maisie's father. As Mrs. Beale, his second wife, she meets, in Maisie's interest, the mother's second husband, Sir Claude, and Maisie promptly catches at 'the pleasant possibility, in connection with herself, of a relation much happier as between Mrs. Beale and Sir Claude than as between mamma and papa'. The step-parents do indeed fall in love, thus making the 'fresh system of misbehaviour', and are gradually estranged from their spouses. The latter, Maisie's original parents, take up with other lovers and leave her more and more to the care of her step-father and step-mother.

Meanwhile Maisie's mother has engaged a second governess, Mrs. Wix, as old and dowdy and high-principled as Miss Overmore was young and pretty and light; and as Beale and Ida fade from the picture we are left with a foursome: Maisie, her step-parents and her governess. Maisie loves all three of them, and is herself genuinely loved by the resolute Mrs. Wix and the irresolute Sir Claude. Sir Claude is loved by both women, but by now is deeply entangled with Mrs. Beale, who pretends to love Maisie in order to hang on to him. Mrs. Wix and Mrs. Beale are at daggers drawn in their jealousy over both Maisie and Sir Claude, and the story reaches its climax as the two women fight for possession of the man and the girl. Both want both, but in the end Mrs. Wix gets Maisie and Mrs. Beale gets Sir Claude.

During the week at Boulogne which is the scene of this struggle, James contrives a series of combinations between Maisie and the other three characters which enables the final drama of their relations to be shown in its complexity. First Sir Claude brings Maisie over from Folkestone and they are alone together in unclouded happiness; then Mrs. Wix arrives, darkening the sky with her moral imperatives; then Sir Claude returns to England, summoned by Mrs. Beale, and leaves Maisie to Mrs. Wix; then Mrs. Beale comes over alone to assert her rights over Maisie and to 'square' Mrs. Wix; then Sir Claude rejoins them, the four come together briefly and passionately, and the situation is finally resolved.

This series of actual scenes is matched by the series of possible solutions for Maisie which come up in turn for consideration:

—that Maisie should live with all three of them; (This is the ideal solution, and what Maisie would like—'Why shouldn't we be four?' she asks—but the two women could never endure it.)

—that Maisie should live with Sir Claude and Mrs. Wix; (This is what Mrs. Wix wants: both she and Maisie 'adore' Sir Claude, and she wants to save him from his adulterous connection with the 'bad' Mrs. Beale; but Sir Claude cannot give up Mrs. Beale.)

—that Maisie should live with Sir Claude and Mrs. Beale; (This is what Sir Claude and Mrs. Beale want, but Maisie will not give up Mrs. Wix.)

—that Maisie should go off alone with Sir Claude; (This is her 'ultimatum' to Sir Claude: she will give up Mrs. Wix only if he will give up Mrs. Beale; but he can't, unless Mrs Beale gives *him* up, which she won't.)

—that Maisie should fall to Mrs. Wix, and Sir Claude to Mrs. Beale. (This is the eventual solution, and its inevitability has gradually become apparent over the final pages. No one is left out, alone, and each of the 'hard' characters, Mrs. Wix and Mrs. Beale, gets possession of one of the 'soft' characters, Maisie and Sir Claude.)

James's feeling for 'a proper symmetry' expresses itself both in what actually happens—correspondences between characters and events, as in what he called 'pendant-scenes'—and in the way the characters, and Maisie not least, canvass the possible permutations among themselves—a canvassing of which the above is only the most elaborate example. *His* use of symmetry for giving shapeliness to the story is a device, common in narrative art, upon which he refines in a characteristic manner. (He makes, for example, two important 'pendant-scenes' of two occasions when Maisie, out with one of her step-parents, meets that parent's spouse, her real father or mother, in the company of a new lover. In each case there is an explosion of jealousy and resentment, though the consequences, for Maisie, are very different. The Notebooks show how James reduced the symmetry of detail in the two scenes from his first intention, so as to make them less artificial and at the same time richer in their repercussions.) *Their* frequent sense of how this moment or person resembles that, how one situation recalls or implies another, springs from an awareness of life's many possibilities and from their desire to find a meaning in their predicament.

But James developed his plot above all for the sake of his heroine. The story's centre of interest was to be her 'small expanding consciousness', and he saw that the six-year-old Maisie, bandied from one parent to the other and loved by neither, began life at such a disadvantage that her consciousness might well be merely 'coarsened, blurred, sterilised, by ignorance and pain'. He developed the plot, with its second marriages and the consequent coming together of the step-parents over the child, as a way of providing her with a 'better state', and making her 'presentable as a register of impressions'. However, Sir Claude and Mrs. Beale are brought together not by Maisie's mere existence, but by her charm, by 'the strange, fatal, complicating action of the child's lovability'. Maisie is in an extraordinary predicament, and she must be an extraordinary person to match it, able to survive and even to profit from situations that might leave a more ordinary child at a loss.

Stories that feature the baneful psychological effects of a child's deprivation of parental affection and lack of a settled home are two a penny. James appears to have consciously ignored the probability that what Maisie suffers would make her thoroughly disturbed, psychologically sick. As his heroes and heroines habitually do, she preserves her equanimity and good humour unscathed, and thus triumphs, morally, over her disadvantages. A passage from the Preface explains the importance he attached to this achievement of hers:

> No themes are so human as those that reflect for us, out of the confusion of life, the close connection of bliss and bale, of the things that help with the things that hurt . . .

It would be Maisie's fate

> to live with all intensity and perplexity and felicity in her terribly mixed little world, really keeping the torch of virtue alive in an air tending infinitely to smother it; really in short making confusion worse confounded by drawing some stray fragrance of an ideal across the scent of selfishness, by sowing on barren strands, through the mere fact of presence, the seed of the moral life.

He saw his adult characters as mostly deplorable. As he wrote of the scene in Kensington Gardens (Chs. 15–16):

> The human substance here would have seemed in advance wellnigh too poor for conversion, the three 'mature' figures of too short a radiation, too stupid (*so* stupid it was for Sir Claude to have married Ida!), too vain, too thin, for any clear application; but promptly, immediately, the child's own importance, spreading and contagiously acting, has determined the *total* value otherwise.

However, this is not to say that James disregards all psychological probability in the presentation of his heroine. Accepting the general premiss that Maisie shall survive and even profit from her experience, we can see that there is a great deal of psychological subtlety and truth in the detail of her reactions. Here she is, for example, at the age of six, having impressed upon her by her nurse Moddle her father's fiction that he has made great sacrifices for her:

> She was familiar, at the age of six, with the fact that everything had been changed on her account, everything ordered to enable him to give himself up to her. She was to remember always the words in which Moddle impressed upon her that he did so give himself: 'Your papa wishes you never to forget, you know, that he has been dreadfully put about.' If the skin on Moddle's face had to Maisie the air of being unduly, almost painfully, stretched, it never presented that appearance so much as when she uttered, as she often had occasion to utter, such words. The child wondered if they didn't make it hurt more than usual . . .   Ch. 1, p. 22

This passage is not just an account of the idea Maisie was presented with, but an imaginative entry into her point of view. For her, Moddle's words were inseparable from the way they were spoken: the painful stretching of her skin might seem irrelevant, a child's arbitrary association, but when Maisie wonders if the words 'didn't make it hurt more than usual', we see that this is her childlike approach to a sense that appearance is expressive, and that Moddle's face looks as it does either because she speaks with unusual severity or, more likely, because it expresses the awkwardness she feels at dutifully repeating the words of her employer, and her embarrassment at their hypocrisy. Appropriately, the point is not clarified, since for Maisie it was no more than a dim, perplexed intimation; but by making the image in her mind suggest a little more to us than it does to Maisie herself, James both marks the present limits of her understanding and shows, in her curious observation of appearances, the ground of its future development. Having made as much as that out of the small particular instance, James has earned the right to pass on to generalisation as he immediately does:

> . . . but it was only after some time that she was able to attach to the picture of her father's sufferings, and more particularly to her nurse's manner about them, the meaning for which these things had waited. By the time she had grown sharper, as the gentlemen who criticised her calves used to say, she found in her mind a collection of

images and echoes to which meanings were attachable—images and echoes kept for her in the childish dusk, the dim closet, the high drawers, like games she wasn't yet big enough to play. The great strain meanwhile was that of carrying by the right end the things her father said about her mother—things mostly indeed that Moddle, on a glimpse of them, as if they had been complicated toys or difficult books, took out of her hands and put away in the closet. A wonderful assortment of objects of this kind she was later to discover there, all tumbled up too with the things, shuffled into the same receptacle, that her mother had said about her father.

The generalisations here are vivified by a selection of images appropriate to Maisie's experience and serving to stress, by likening ideas to toys, the way in which for young children the moral life is all entangled with the physical.

Another general point about her growing up is similarly grounded in the detail of her peculiar life. This is the fact that gradually the naïve candour of the very young, revealing everything, is overlaid by the discovery that they can keep things to themselves. Upon this discovery, whose use is for a proper privacy and whose abuse is lying and deceit, depends the development of the inner life, and by extension the possibility of civilised living. In Chapter 2 James presents this discovery on Maisie's part as a 'moral revolution', dependent on 'a great date in her small still life'. For two years she has been the innocent carrier of insults between her father and mother. It first occurs to her that she might do otherwise when her governess, Miss Overmore, asks her not to tell her mother that they have been meeting her father. Thereupon:

The stiff little dolls on the dusky shelves began to move their arms and legs; old forms and phrases began to have a sense that frightened her. She had a new feeling, the feeling of danger; on which a new remedy rose to meet it, the idea of an inner self or, in other words, of concealment. She puzzled out with imperfect signs, but with a prodigious spirit, that she had been a centre of hatred and a messenger of insult, and that everything was bad because she had been employed to make it so. Her parted lips locked themselves with the determination to be employed no longer. She would forget everything, she would repeat nothing, and when, as a tribute to the successful application of her system, she began to be called a little idiot, she tasted a pleasure new and keen. When therefore, as she grew older, her parents in turn announced that she had grown shockingly dull, it was not from any real contraction of her little stream of life. She spoiled their fun, but she practically added to her own. She saw more and more; she saw too much.

Ch. 2, p. 25

Psychologically there is a convincing balance between the prompting she receives from outside and the extent of her initiative in acting upon it.

'She saw too much . . .' In her 'sharpened sense of spectatorship' Maisie resembles many Jamesian heroes and heroines, condemned to see more than those around them see, and at the same time to act less. There is a moral quality in the seeing, and if you see as much as that, you have an amount of moral imagination that may well unfit you for action. By necessity largely passive in an adult world, Maisie makes the most of her restriction, epitomising such adult characters as Hyacinth Robinson (*The Princess Casamassima*), Fleda Vetch (*The Spoils of Poynton*), Lambert Strether (*The Ambassadors*) and Maggie Verver (*The Golden Bowl*). These are all 'good' characters and 'soft' characters, deeply involved, emotionally, in the lives of other less good, sometimes positively bad and always less perceptive characters, but more or less excluded from the latter's full confidence, kept at arm's length, and mystified. Moreover they are conscious of this role they play:

> So the sharpened sense of spectatorship was the child's main support, the long habit, from the first, of seeing herself in discussion and finding in the fury of it—she had had a glimpse of the game of football—a sort of compensation for the doom of a peculiar passivity. It gave her often an odd air of being present at her history in as separate a manner as if she could only get at experience by flattening her nose against a pane of glass.   Ch. 12, p. 83

This makes the essential points: that the spectator is deeply involved ('seeing herself in discussion'), and finds in that a compensation 'for the doom of a peculiar passivity'.

On the subject of Sir Claude and Mrs. Beale coming together over Maisie, James wrote in his Notebook the words 'Description of it in form of picture of her dim sense'. This phrase sounds needlessly elaborate, but is not. Our opportunities to learn of their liaison are no greater than Maisie's: we see no more of it than she sees. But she sees more than she understands, and we understand more than she does, or at least more quickly. She has a 'dim sense', and the narrative presents directly everything in her experience that contributes to that sense—both what she sees and hears, and what she thinks. All this constitutes the substance of the narrative. But the *terms* of the narrative are not Maisie's own:

> Small children have many more perceptions than they have terms to translate them; their vision is at any moment much richer, their apprehension even constantly stronger, than their prompt, their at all producible, vocabulary. Amusing therefore as it might at the first blush have seemed to restrict myself in this case to the terms as well as to the experience, it became at once plain that such an attempt would fail. Maisie's terms accordingly play their part— since her simpler conclusions quite depend on them; but our own commentary constantly attends and amplifies.   Preface

Thus the important developments in the story (that her parents don't love her, that they begin to find supporting her a bore, that Sir Claude and Mrs. Beale become clandestine lovers, that Mrs. Beale is less fond of Maisie than she professes, that Sir Claude is good but terribly weak, etc.) are described not simply *through* her 'dim sense' of them—as would be the case if the story took the form of a first-person narrative told by Maisie. Her sense of them is presented objectively, as something placed and framed by the author's commentary, which 'constantly attends and amplifies', and by our understanding more than, or something different from, what Maisie herself understands. Hence the phrase 'in form of *picture* of her dim sense'.

This method allows ironical effects that would hardly be possible by the simpler method of first-person narration. We see much more than Maisie does of how things are going between Sir Claude and Mrs. Beale and how Mrs. Wix tries to interfere;

but we see without benefit of any evidence not available to her, and measure thereby our own fallen, knowing, adult state, our own distance from the innocence of childhood. In this respect we stand beside the corrupt adults, not beside Maisie. Yet there's a difference between our reactions and theirs to what she sees and says and understands. Helped by the author's commentary, we know more of this than they do; and though often, with them, we are amazed or amused by her, yet not being personally involved, we don't share their embarrassment at what she sometimes comes out with.

Thus when Maisie comes in to find Sir Claude paying a first visit to Mrs. Beale, the way they're getting on together makes her wonder what her father would think if he knew of Sir Claude's visit:

> 'Have you seen papa?' she asked of Sir Claude.
>
> It was the signal for their going off again, as her small stoicism had perfectly taken for granted that it would be. All that Mrs. Beale had nevertheless to add was the vague apparent sarcasm: 'Oh papa!'
>
> 'I'm assured he's not at home,' Sir Claude replied to the child; 'but if he had been I should have hoped for the pleasure of seeing him.'
>
> 'Won't he mind your coming?' Maisie asked as with need of the knowledge.
>
> 'Oh you bad little girl!' Mrs. Beale humorously protested.
>
> The child could see that at this Sir Claude, though still moved to mirth, coloured a little; but he spoke to her very kindly. 'That's just what I came to see, you know—whether your father *would* mind.'
>
> Ch. 8, p. 54

Maisie has long been familar with the way one adult in her life inexplicably takes against another. The ground of the objection, sexual jealousy, she is too young to understand, but her question brings it up for Sir Claude and Mrs. Beale, and for us. Mrs. Beale is embarrassed, but laughs it off with a retort—'Oh you bad little girl!'—which is both wholly unjust and obscure to Maisie. It is then Sir Claude's turn to be embarrassed—by Maisie's question but also, we divine, by Mrs. Beale's disingenuous reception of it. Without any direct statement by the author, the brief exchange has revealed, in dramatic terms, the moral distance between Maisie and the two grown-ups, and also between Mrs. Beale and Sir Claude—he is fairer and finer than she. James has given us the chance to notice all this while we stay with Maisie and see just what she sees: Sir Claude's embarrassment, which she doesn't understand, and his kindliness.

Similar comic irony arises from the euphemisms and vagueness of the grown-ups in referring to what they would be embarrassed to name more explicitly. Thus Sir Claude tells Maisie he has 'squared' her mother, and when this leaves her blank he explains:

> 'I mean that your mother lets me do what I want so long as I let her do what *she* wants.'
> 'So you *are* doing what you want?' Maisie asked.
> 'Rather, Miss Farange!'
> Miss Farange turned it over. 'And she's doing the same?'
> 'Up to the hilt!'
> Again she considered. 'Then, please, what may it be?'
> 'I wouldn't tell you for the whole world.'   Ch. 13, p. 87

What Sir Claude means is that Ida won't object to his carrying on with Mrs. Beale if he'll turn a blind eye to her own intrigues. This is beyond Maisie, but she remembers the terms and when, in the next chapter, Mrs. Beale comes out with the remark that she has 'squared' Maisie's father,

> '*I* know how!' Maisie was prompt to proclaim. 'By letting him do what he wants on condition that he lets you also do it.'
> 'You're too delicious, my own pet!'—she was involved in another hug. 'How in the world have I got on so long without you?'
>   Ch. 14, p. 96

Maisie is right here, though she doesn't fully understand what she is right about, and the euphemism is vague enough for Mrs. Beale to enjoy it—but her patronising comment is characteristic: Sir Claude is the only adult who treats Maisie as an equal and with full love.

Characterisation of the adults is done externally. By and large, we see no more of them than Maisie sees, and so they are revealed mostly in their relations with her. James would never let into the book itself the sort of summary authorial judgment on a character that we find in the Notebooks, where he says of Sir Claude, for example, that he has a 'pretty, pleasant, weak, bullied, finally disgusted nature'. In the book itself such 'facts' about a character do sometimes come out in conversation, and towards the end of the story Maisie is becoming more capable of general reflection, so that we get such a passage as the long second paragraph of Chapter 30, where the splendid description of her breakfast in the café with Sir Claude passes on to her noticing his peculiar nervousness, and from there to what is almost a general judgment on the man but remains something more subtle as it falls back into the context of the present moment:

> She had seen him nervous, she had seen everyone she had come in contact with nervous, but she had never seen him so nervous as this. Little by little it gave her a settled terror, a terror that partook of the coldness she had felt just before, at the hotel, to find herself, on his answer about Mrs. Beale, disbelieve him. She seemed to see at present, to touch across the table, as if by laying her hand on it, what he had meant when he confessed on those several occasions to fear. Why was such a man so often afraid? It must have begun to come to her now that there was one thing just such a man above all could be afraid of. He could be afraid of himself. His fear at all events was there; his fear was sweet to her, beautiful and tender to her, was having coffee and buttered rolls and talk and laughter that were no talk and laughter at all with her; his fear was in his jesting postponing perverting voice ... Ch. 30, p. 223

The passage is typical of James's masterful integration, especially in his later works, of general points into the texture of the narrative. In other novelists—George Eliot or Hardy, for example—they often stand out blatantly as author's comment in a special author's tone of voice; in James they spring from the characters' experience of the moment. What T. S. Eliot said of the integrity of James's own mind—'He had a mind so fine that no idea could violate it'—could be adapted to the integrity of his narrative: 'It has a texture so fine that no idea can violate it.'

Maisie herself is presented both externally and from within.

Were she not presented externally, in word and action, we should not appreciate her charm. We must see her partly as the other characters see her, be treated, as they are, to 'the rich little spectacle of objects embalmed in her wonder', and then we shall understand what they do for her. Her father and mother do nothing and are thereby condemned; Mrs. Beale, to the very end, '*really* clings to her—partly from her old affection, the charm of the child ... and partly because her presence is a way of *attracting* Sir Claude and making a tie *with* him' (Notebooks, p. 261)— and is thus placed as unscrupulous but not wholly selfish; Sir Claude and Mrs. Wix are genuinely devoted to her in their different ways. But Maisie's moral life is filled out for us from within. The way this is done may be illustrated by a close look at two short passages.

The first is a sentence from Chapter 20. Maisie has been brusquely carried off to Folkestone by Sir Claude and 'established at a lovely hotel'. He has been persuaded to this by Mrs. Wix, who has long sought to disentangle him from Mrs. Beale, whom she is passionately jealous of and regards as a wicked woman. What Mrs. Wix has been able to play on is Sir Claude's reluctance to involve Maisie in the impropriety of his liaison. The sentence in which this point is made reads as follows:

> I may not even answer for it that Maisie was not aware of how, in this, Mrs. Beale failed to share his all but insurmountable distaste for their allowing their little charge to breathe the air of their gross irregularity—his contention, in a word, that they should either cease to be irregular or cease to be parental. Ch. 20, p. 146

The essential information is given in the words 'his all but insurmountable distaste for their allowing their little charge to breathe the air of their gross irregularity'. (This is already characteristically Jamesian, with the descriptive periphrasis of 'their little charge', referring to Maisie, and the vagueness, whether for decorum or for its moral suggestiveness, of 'their gross irregularity', referring to Sir Claude's double adultery with Mrs. Beale.) The involvement he wishes to avoid is expressed metaphorically: Maisie must not be allowed to '*breathe*

the air . . .'. But there is no question of James letting this idea stand on its own, as a fact communicated directly by narrator to reader. The latter must come at it as Maisie did, that is to say as the reason for Sir Claude's carrying her off in a great hurry, without telling Mrs. Beale and giving her the chance to prevent it. So we get '. . . Maisie was . . . aware of how, in this, Mrs. Beale failed to share his all but insurmountable distaste . . .'. But even this is more direct than James is prepared to be, and so we get the further elaboration of the full sentence as it stands in the text: 'I may not even answer for it that Maisie was not aware of how . . .' Is this last complicating uncertainty justifiable? Why shouldn't the narrator just *know* what Maisie was aware of? The answer is that children *are* often only dimly aware, and that the question of what she is and is not aware of is the very subject of the book, as its title proclaims. Maisie could never have expressed such a complicated idea as James here wants to suggest that she apprehends. As he says on the previous page, 'She had ever in her mind fewer names than conceptions'. So his elaboration can be justified on grounds of realism.

The second example comes two pages later. Maisie is still at Folkestone, sitting with Sir Claude in the hotel garden before dinner:

> Adjusting her respirations and attaching, under dropped lashes, all her thought to a smartness of frock and frill for which she could reflect that she had not appealed in vain to a loyalty in Susan Ash triumphant over the nice things their feverish flight had left behind, Maisie spent on a bench in the garden of the hotel the half-hour before dinner, that mysterious ceremony of the *table d'hôte* for which she had prepared with a punctuality of flutter.
>
> Ch. 20, p. 148

The sentence gathers in some of Maisie's experience of the day: the 'feverish flight' from London; how there was no time to pack more than a few clothes, but how Susan Ash helped her to include something smart; how Susan was loyal to Maisie—she might not have been, since she was in the employ of Beale and Mrs. Beale, and in helping Maisie now she was being disloyal to her employers. (This little moral complication is touched on only in this sentence, as something upon which Maisie 'could reflect' after the event, that is to say, not as a fact in itself but as part of Maisie's experience. What more likely than that at such a moment of calm, while Sir Claude sits beside her 'occupied with a cigarette and the afternoon papers', Maisie should think back over the day and consider such a matter as how Susan responded to the emergency?)

These recollections and reflections of Maisie's are not given us just loosely in the context of her sitting in the hotel garden: James relates them to her consciousness of her present appearance, adequately smart for dinner. Yet this could have been done more simply than he does it: he might have written 'Looking at her frilled frock, for the smartness of which she could reflect . . .'. The further complication of what he actually wrote relates her thoughts to her physical sensations of the moment: 'Adjusting her respirations . . .' This phrase is a good beginning to the sentence—it expresses the quality of the moment, one of adjustment after breathless bustle and excitement. And we are also given a glimpse of Maisie from the outside—'under dropped lashes'—which ties up with the 'smartness of frock and frill' and the further detail of the scene in the main clause. (Why not 'looking at her smart frilled frock'? Because the frock only comes into the scene at all because Maisie is concerned about whether it's smart enough for dinner: it's not the frock itself but its smartness that matters to her.)

This sentence is a fairly extreme example of the general tendency of James's writing to relate one thing with another instead of presenting them separately. His later style developed to perform this function more fully, becoming elaborately hypotactic, with complex subordinate clauses, and making much use of qualification—by relative clauses, apposition, etc.—to bring in further aspects of the whole: not just 'her smartness of frock and frill', but 'a smartness . . . *for which* she could reflect . . .'. James presents as a coherent whole a range of facts—physical, intellectual, moral, emotional—that are indeed all related in the heroine's experience, but are not easily related by someone writing *about* that experience. Life *is* complicated, and to render the texture of it moment by moment is a complicated business.

The moral issues the story raises are presented in a similar way to the various facts and ideas in the two sentences just analysed, that is to say, with all the vagueness of principle and directness of personal application with which the child herself apprehends them. The scene between Maisie and Mrs. Wix at Boulogne, in Chapter 25, comes as near as anything, under Mrs. Wix's insistence, to dotting the i's and crossing the t's of the immorality that Maisie is to be 'saved' from. The moral principle comes very close to explicit statement, but it never actually gets there because for Maisie, and for James, perhaps, it remains a matter just of personal relations, of the particular case. She insists on the freedom of Sir Claude and Mrs. Beale, now that her father and mother have gone off in open rupture. For Maisie, this is the freedom to be with those you love, to follow the heart's affections. The only bars to such freedom, in her view, are personal involvement with another, and there seems none left now to confine them. For Mrs. Wix, their 'freedom' is a matter of convention: however final the rupture, Sir Claude is still Ida's husband, as Mrs. Beale is Beale's wife, and convention says they are not free to live together, so if they insist on doing so they must be made to give Maisie up. The exchange with Mrs Wix goes:

> '. . . Well, if Sir Claude's old enough to know better, upon my word I think it's right to treat you as if you also were . . . Free, free, free? If she's as free as *you* are, my dear, she's free enough, to be sure!'
>
> 'As I am?'—Maisie, after reflexion and despite whatever of portentous this seemed to convey, risked a critical echo.
>
> 'Well,' said Mrs. Wix, 'nobody, you know, is free to commit a crime.'
>
> 'A crime!' The word had come out in a way that made the child sound it again.
>
> 'You'd commit as great a one as their own—and so should I—if we were to condone their immorality by our presence.'

Maisie waited a little; this seemed so fiercely conclusive. 'Why is it immorality?' she nevertheless presently inquired.

Her companion now turned upon her with a reproach softer because it was somehow deeper. 'You're too unspeakable! Do you know what we're talking about?'

In the interest of ultimate calm Maisie felt that she must be above all clear. 'Certainly; about their taking advantage of their freedom.'

'Well, to do what?'

'Why, to live with us.'

Mrs. Wix's laugh, at this, was literally wild. ' "Us"? Thank you!'

'Then to live with *me*.'   Ch. 25, p. 189

This is a splendidly comic but also serious moment. We smile at Maisie's failure to grasp the matter of principle—which is of course the very ground of Mrs. Wix's stand—that they are not morally free to live together in sin. We also smile at, and admire and applaud, the consistency with which Maisie clings to the particular case ('to live with us', 'to live with *me*') and bases her morality upon it, empirically. We know, too, that Mrs. Wix is moved by other, personal considerations: she loves Sir Claude and cannot bear the idea of sharing him with Mrs. Beale. But Maisie can see them all together as a foursome: 'Stay on as just what you were at mamma's. Mrs. Beale *would* let you!' Maisie shows up here as naïve—Mrs. Beale *wouldn't* let her—but as generous too. Under Mrs. Wix's instruction she has come, we surmise, to know what's going on between Sir Claude and Mrs. Beale, or at least to know that by the world's standard of morality it won't do. But she has learned to know without learning to condemn. The scene in which her governess taxes her with this (Ch. 26), with Maisie on the balcony of the hotel, open to the influences of the summer night and the manners of France in the street and the café below, while Mrs. Wix stays firmly inside the room and sticks to her moral guns, is a fine instance of how James can use a descriptive passage to dramatise a moral issue. It might be compared with Chapters 3 and 4 of Book XI of *The Ambassadors*, where Strether meets Chad and Mme. de Vionnet on the river, and with Chapter 7 of 'Madame de Mauves', where Longmore wanders off into the country and observes the young French painter with his mistress at the inn.

Knowing, but refusing to condemn, Maisie now has the intelligence of a woman, but unlike the women in her own life, Mrs. Wix included, she is neither prejudiced nor possessive. It could indeed be said that she is a heroine in the old sense, an ideal figure rather than a real one. No real girl ever combined what Maisie combines. But she is not a sentimental creation, an idle pipe-dream. In imagining such a figure, such a combination, James has a serious artistic and critical purpose. She is worked out consistently in the full detail of what such a combination involves and how a human being possessed of it would find herself engaged with the crudities and hypocrisies of adult life in a fallen world. James found for his novel a situation in which such a figure would stand out in sharpest relief against the moral obliquities of the grown-ups. Maisie is the still centre round which they more or less grotesquely turn. As James put it in his Preface:

> She has the wonderful importance of shedding a light far beyond any reach of her comprehension; of lending to poorer persons and things, by the mere fact of their being involved with her and by the special scale she creates for them, a precious element of dignity. I lose myself, truly, in appreciation of my theme on noting what she does by her 'freshness' for appearances in themselves vulgar and empty enough. They become, as she deals with them, the stuff of poetry and tragedy and art; she has simply to wonder, as I say, about them, and they begin to have meanings, aspects, solidities, connexions—connexions with the 'universal!'—that they could scarce have hoped for.

The book is a delight to read, and frequently hilarious. The style is not always as elaborate as the two sentences chosen for analysis above. James can write a short sentence with a neatly balanced, witty turn of phrase, as when he says, of Maisie's parents, 'Their rupture had resounded, and after being perfectly insignificant together they would be decidedly striking apart', or when he mentions her early realisation that 'the natural way for a child to have her parents was separate and successive, like her mutton and her pudding or her bath and her nap'. He can throw in the sort of extra, unexpected descriptive touch one associates rather with Dickens, as when Maisie's father and Miss Overmore, fetching her back from her mother's, have 'a merry little scrimmage' over her in the brougham, 'of which Maisie caught the surprised perception in the white stare of an old lady who passed in a victoria'.

There is much fine comic characterisation. Ida, whose face is likened to 'an illuminated garden, turnstile and all, for the frequentation of which he had his season-ticket', is magnificently atrocious in her last scene with Maisie, pouring out her transparently bogus excuses and nauseating self-pity with the fluency and elaboration of syntax that James allows to all his characters. Sir Claude is a specially fruity example of the comic use James makes of the vagueness of English upper-class idiom and the way it's used as a substitute for precise thought or direct statement (cf. as early a story as the excellent 'International Episode', of 1878). Once he says to Maisie:

> 'We probably shouldn't give you another governess. To begin with we shouldn't be able to get one—not of the only kind that would do. It wouldn't do—the kind that *would* do,' he queerly enough explained. 'I mean they wouldn't stay—heigh-ho! We'd do you ourselves. Particularly me. You see I *can* now; I haven't got to mind—what I used to. I won't fight shy as I did—she can show out *with* me. Our relation, all round, is more regular.'
>
> Ch. 30, p. 231

Mrs. Wix, to the end, is a marvellous mixture of the absurd and the admirable. She speaks with real moral authority, and we feel it right, though hard luck for Maisie, that she gets the child in the end, but comically it's right for other reasons than those she so confidently professes.

We may value the novel also as a picture of a social group—whose morals, incidentally, are such as no other English novelist of the period would probably have dared to treat. Superficially, the background is the same as that of *The Awkward Age*, published two years later: idle upper-class Londoners who dine out most nights of the week and spend weekends in the country. But in *The Awkward Age* all the characters are right inside that social world, so we get a picture of it from within. Besides, the main characters are rather special people, highly intelligent and sophisticated, and form a special group with its own rarefied atmosphere inside the larger social context. In *What Maisie Knew* that world is seen from the outside, with some of its untidy fringes: Maisie is too young to have the entrée, and lives with nursemaids and governesses; Miss Overmore is on the edge, doing her best to scramble in; Beale is gradually dropping out; and no one in the book could conceivably have been admitted to the charmed circle of Mrs. Brook.

If the book is harder to read as it goes along, this is because Maisie grows up and life gets more complicated for her. There is a kind of compensation for the increasing complexity, in the increasing pace of the story. The first half of the book covers her life from the age of six to one that's never stated but that we take to be about ten, eleven or twelve. She is already eight after about ten pages, and there is a gradual intensification of incident—scenes becoming longer and the gaps between them shorter—up to Chapter 17, when the single day of the visit to Earls Court and her last scene with her father occupies twenty pages. Then Sir Claude carries her off to Folkestone, and from then every day counts. The second half of the book covers only a week, and the last quarter only twenty-four hours. Time goes by more slowly, but that's because more is packed into it, and the pace of the narrative quickens to an exciting climax.

This short work is the most accessible of James's later novels: clear in outline, coherent in construction, and consistently entertaining. It is also serious and profound, dealing with subjects that concern us all: childhood and the end of childhood; parental affection, its failure and its substitutes. Beneath the comic surface there lurk, as Maisie saw for her mother, 'madness and desolation, . . . ruin and darkness and death'; but the story is one of how these horrors are kept at bay by innocence and intelligence, good humour and imagination.

7

The Tales

James's one hundred and twelve short stories, or tales, as they are perhaps more appropriately called, vary in length from about twenty to a hundred and twenty pages. The longest of them, such as 'A London Life' or 'The Turn of the Screw', are little shorter than his shortest novels, and we need a word to distinguish these from the really short stories that are barely a fifth as long. The French, Germans and Russians all have a word for fictions of this length; we have only the unsatisfactory term 'long short story'. James himself frequently used the French word *nouvelle*, and lamented that stories of this length were unpopular with English editors.

The tales begin to be worth re-reading from about 'Madame de Mauves' (1874) onwards. James produced first-class work in the genre for over thirty years, and the twelve volumes of the current edition represent a major literary achievement which any writer might be proud to have given his working life to. It has been matched only by Chekhov. The fact that James once referred to his tales as 'little tarts'—his novels constituting the 'beef and potatoes'—should not lead anyone to suppose that they are not frequently profound, as well as consistently brilliant.

With his interest in narrative technique and his desire that works of fiction should be coherent and shapely, it is not surprising that James should have been attracted by the problems of the short narrative. He never found it easy to be really brief: his Notebooks show again and again how a story would grow, under his pen, far beyond its planned dimensions. But he went on trying for brevity. He described 'the very short story' as 'one of the costliest, even if, like the hard, shining sonnet, one of the most indestructible, forms of composition in general use' (Preface to 'The Author of Beltraffio'). The comparison with poetry is suggestive. A really short story is not just a novel in miniature. For one thing, it cannot create, as a novel can, a whole social world of its own. For another, whether or not the narrator is distinct from the author and involved in the action, the reader is often conscious of his voice establishing a strongly felt narrative 'mode'. The modern short story, as it developed in the 19th century, could be said to derive from the ancient tradition of popular *oral* narrative.

With respect to method of narration, James's tales can be divided into three categories: those told by a narrator in the first person; those told in the third person from the point of view of a single observer (occasionally two of these), and those in which the narration is 'free', confined to no particular point of view. Most of his tales belong to the first two categories.

Although James thought it undesirable to have a first-person narrator for a full-length novel (see Preface to *The Ambassadors*), he used this device in more than a third of his tales, including two of his best known works, 'The Aspern Papers' and 'The Turn of the Screw'. In some of these stories the narrator is a mere observer. He witnesses the action of the story, and communicates with those who act and suffer, but does not himself take part. In others he is more involved in the action, and in some he is a principal, or *the* principal, agent. In any case, however much of a mere observer the narrator may be, he is not the author, not James. He cannot, as the author can, 'go behind' any of the characters, enter their consciousness and exhibit it from the inside. The story is told strictly from his point of view, and in his words. This imposes a filter between the reader and the events described. Such a story is far removed from drama, where there is no narrative filter at all, and from the novel written in the third person, in which the author 'goes behind' the characters, or at least the main ones, and can give information to the reader about the scene and the events from a position of detached omniscience. The narrative of such a story is thus peculiarly subjective: we see and hear only what the narrator sees and hears. His view is our view because no other view is given. Yet his view is partial, limited by circumstance and opportunity, and also by the sort of person he is, his interest and his intelligence. The quality of these can be expressed by the style of the narration, and we may be conscious of this style, react to it, and even dissociate ourselves from it. Without direct interference, the author may be able to make us see more than the narrator sees.

Not many tales have a first-person narrator deeply involved in the action. Two notable exceptions, 'The Aspern Papers' and 'The Turn of the Screw', are perhaps distinguished by the narrator's being wrong or deluded. What is not suitable is to have a hero tell his own story if he's too good, too wise, too much in the right. Modesty requires that such a story be told by another.

The tales told in the third person from the point of view of a single character are, with respect to narrative technique, similar to such a novel as *The Spoils of Poynton*, *What Maisie Knew* or *The Ambassadors*. I have discussed what James makes of this method on pages 108–10 and 112-16 above.

With respect to subject, I find almost all the tales I most admire can be grouped under four heads:

1. International tales, concentrating on the 'mixture of manners' when Americans meet Europeans. Most of these are light and comic, were written between 1874 and 1888, and were among his most popular works. They include 'Madame de Mauves', 'Four Meetings', 'Daisy Miller', 'An International Episode', 'The Pension Beaurepas', 'A Bundle of Letters', 'The Point of View', 'The Siege of London', 'Lady Barberina', 'Pandora' and 'Miss Gunton of Poughkeepsie'.

2. Tales about the life of artists, the connexions between art and life, and the related subject of the invasion of privacy—often a writer's privacy—by the press or some other public interest. These tales mostly belong to James's middle period, the late eighties and the nineties. They are often sharply satirical and bitterly comic, expressing his increasing gloom at the absence, at least in Anglo-Saxon countries, of any proper understanding of art and the artist. He tackled the subject of the artist in con-temporary society in a novel of this period, *The Tragic Muse*

(1890). In its Preface he wrote: 'Art indeed has in our day taken on so many honours and emoluments that the recognition of its importance is more than a custom, has become on occasion almost a fury: the line is drawn—especially in the English world —only at the importance of heeding what it may mean.'

3. Tales about children and parents, and the demands one generation makes upon another. These belong to the same period as the second group. In several of them the young are victims of their elders' indifference, or their excessive demands. In either case there is a failure of sympathy and understanding, sometimes with tragic consequences. This group of tales includes 'Louisa Pallant', 'The Pupil', 'The Marriages', 'The Chaperon', ' Owen Wingrave', 'The Turn of the Screw' and ' "Europe" '. Three novels of the late nineties, *What Maisie Knew*, *The Awkward Age* and *The Ambassadors*, also treat aspects of this subject.

4. Lastly, tales of the middle-aged or the elderly. After a life more or less misspent in drudgery, dissipation or exile, they take stock of what they have missed and, in some cases, find unexpected companionship and sympathy as they face what's left to come. These tales, foreshadowed by the case of Lambert Strether, hero of *The Ambassadors*, belong to James's last period. They include some of his very best: 'Broken Wings', 'The Beast in the Jungle', 'The Jolly Corner', 'Crapy Cornelia' and 'The Bench of Desolation'.

Some very good tales that fit into none of these groups are 'The Liar', 'A London Life', 'The Patagonia', 'Brooksmith' and 'In the Cage'.

Unlike some of the best stories of Chekhov and James Joyce, James's tales never aspire to the condition of pure 'picture', presenting an incident which is no more than typical of the life of their subject. They all have a plot and present a drama involving more than one person. Something happens, even if it's mostly a matter of realisation in the mind of the protagonist, and the situation at the end is quite different from what it was at the beginning.

The rest of this chapter examines two tales in some detail.

'The Aspern Papers' belongs to the second group, and 'The Jolly Corner' to the fourth. The third group is represented in this study by *What Maisie Knew*, a story that was meant at first to be short, but burgeoned irresistibly into a novel.

'THE ASPERN PAPERS' (1888)

The unnamed narrator of 'The Aspern Papers' is a scholar and editor. The story of his efforts to lay his hands on some love-letters of a great poet raises questions about the relation between art and life, and measures the gap that yawns ironically between the passionate life of an earlier time, transmuted into lyric art, and the feebler emotions of a more specialised and sophisticated age, bending over the past and trying to discover the secret circumstances of its creativity. Art is public, but the life that created it was private. Should it not remain so? Yet knowledge of the life may illuminate the art, so are we not entitled to find out what we can about it, even if that means exposing to the light of the world documents that were never meant to see it? Or should we take the sterner view that, in T. S. Eliot's words, 'the more perfect the artist, the more completely separate in him will be the man who suffers and the mind which creates'? James's narrator has this out with Miss Bordereau, the guardian of the letters. She asks:

'Do you think it's right to rake up the past?'

'I don't know that I know what you mean by raking it up; but how can we get at it unless we dig a little? The present has such a rough way of treading it down.'

'Oh, I like the past, but I don't like critics,' the old woman declared, with her fine tranquillity.

'Neither do I, but I like their discoveries.'

'Aren't they mostly lies?'

'The lies are what they sometimes discover,' I said, smiling at the quiet impertinence of this. 'They often lay bare the truth.'

'The truth is God's, it isn't man's; we had better leave it alone. Who can judge of it—who can say?'

'We are terribly in the dark, I know,' I admitted; 'but if we give up trying what becomes of all the fine things? What becomes of the work I just mentioned, that of the great philosophers and poets? It is all vain words if there is nothing to measure it by.'

'You talk as if you were a tailor,' said Miss Bordereau . . .

Ch. 7

Clearly, the narrator is exaggerating wildly in his last remark, and deserves her retort. The motives of artistic creation are endlessly mixed and not to be unravelled. What concerns the reader is the charge the words carry, and that depends on what the poet felt, not what he did. It may be said that the life of a great artist is a subject of moral and psychological interest in itself, apart from the study of his work, and thus a legitimate subject for research; but the boundary between art and life remains a doubtful one, a question of knowing, as the narrator says, when to stop. James was writing in the great age of biographical criticism, the age of Sainte-Beuve ('I can enjoy the work itself, but I find it hard to judge it in isolation from the man who wrote it'), and of books like *Shakespeare as an Angler*, *Shakespeare as a Physician*, *Was Shakespeare a Lawyer?*, *Was Not Shakespeare a Gentleman?*, and *Shakespeare, his Inner Life as Intimated in his Works*. In his own literary criticism James constantly fought for a purer approach that should consider the work of art in its own right.

These theoretical questions are sharpened by the circumstances in which they arise in the story. James's narrator is concerned with a recent, 'visitable' past, and the letters are still in the hands of their recipient. His attempt to get hold of them sounds another common theme in James's work, related to that of art and life, namely the invasion of privacy in what is supposedly the larger public interest. He saw this as a peculiarly modern issue, an odious feature of democratic civilisation (see pages 89–91 above). At first the narrator takes an exalted, optimistic view of his intrusion:

My eccentric private errand became a part of the general romance and the general glory—I felt even a mystic companionship, a moral fraternity with all those who in the past had been in the service of art. They had worked for beauty, for a devotion; and what else was I doing? That element was in everything that Jeffrey Aspern had written and I was only bringing it to light.   Ch. 4

Who will say where the service of art ends and that of a prurient curiosity begins? The other view, imputed to Miss Bordereau, is that 'when people want to publish they are capable ... of violating a tomb'.

The hero of 'The Aspern Papers' is in another class than the prying newspaper-men so brilliantly exposed by James elsewhere: he is not after money or fame, but is moved by a genuine interest in his great compatriot, an appreciation of his moral distinction as a man as well as his achievements as an artist. He would not otherwise have been a worthy narrator. Since the whole story comes to us through him, he must be sufficiently perceptive and self-critical to register its morality and sufficiently attractive to enlist our sympathy. We are not left to deduce that he's a 'publishing scoundrel' by his omissions. It is he who tells us at the start that the documents in question are 'personal, delicate, intimate', that 'hypocrisy, duplicity are my only chance', and that he 'felt particularly like the reporter of a newspaper who forces his way into a house of mourning'. He is a sensitive man with the good taste to judge his age—the age, as he says, 'of newspapers and telegrams and photographs and interviewers'. Certainly he is guilty; and though his 'editorial heart' thrills with the idea of the 'esoteric knowledge' Miss Bordereau seems to represent, and he prowls about the great hall of the house hoping for admission to the inner sanctum and 'wondering what mystic rites of ennui the Misses Bordereau celebrated in their darkened rooms', his punishment is to remain literally *profane* (Latin *profanus*: outside the temple), not admitted to the mysteries of the poet he worships. But to call him 'an unfeeling cad' or accuse him of 'a blind egotism that will stop at nothing' is a crude misjudgment. He may not always do the right thing or know when to stop, but he appreciates the virtues and scruples of others even when they obstruct him, and takes a sufficiently critical view of his exploit to narrate its failure with honesty and good humour. (We should not discount from our view of all James's narrators the fact that they themselves have told us their story with elegance, detachment and good humour—a point relevant to the governess who tells the story of 'The Turn of the Screw'. In general, we need to be on our guard against judging James's characters more categorically than he gives us grounds for.)

Psychologically, the narrator is an interesting case of the specialist, whose gifts of intellect and sensibility are concentrated on a single small object, the pursuit of a particular knowledge, that comes to assume an excessive importance in his eyes and blinds him to other values. His failure to allow for the impression he makes on Miss Tita is a consequence of this. The editor is one thing and the man another, and the former flourishes at the latter's expense. The whole is divided, and the editor has no heart—or rather he has a special 'editorial heart'. He lives vicariously off another life in the past more glamorous and passionate than his own, delighting to feel how the papers, now that he and they are under one roof, 'made my life continuous, in a fashion, with the illustrious life they had touched at the other end', and spinning theories about what went on between Miss Bordereau and Jeffrey Aspern while he is himself the unconscious object of an emotion more timid but more actual.

One of the story's fine comic moments occurs when Miss Tita, on learning how much the narrator has done to get the papers, exclaims 'in a candid, wondering way, "How much you must want them!" '—to which he answers, truthfully enough, 'Oh, I do, passionately!' This is one of those moments when the tension of dramatic irony is released as the perceptions of one of the characters at last catch up with what the reader has known for some while. It makes an interesting comparison with the grim moment in *The Portrait of a Lady* when Isabel, at last realising the full force of Osmond's worldy ambition in his desire to secure Lord Warburton for a son-in-law, exclaims:

> 'How much you must want to make sure of him!' . . . She had no sooner spoken than she perceived the full reach of her words, of which she had not been conscious in uttering them. They made a

comparison between Osmond and herself, recalled the fact that she had once held this coveted treasure in her hand and felt herself rich enough to let it fall. A momentary exultation took possession of her—a horrible delight in having wounded him; for his face instantly told her that none of the force of her exclamation was lost. He expressed nothing otherwise, however; he only said quickly: 'Yes, I want it immensely.'   Ch. 46, p. 474

Miss Tita, too, has 'held this coveted treasure in her hand' without suspecting the rate at which it could be prized. But in the tragic context of *The Portrait of a Lady* it is a moment of truth: the characters feel the full implications of their words ('his face instantly told her that none of the force of her exclamation was lost'). In the comic one of 'The Aspern Papers' it is a moment of only relative clarification and there remains a gap, itself a comic effect, between their limited perceptions—Miss Tita has no critical intention and the narrator sees no ground for one—and the reader's.

The corresponding clarification for the narrator occurs after Miss Bordereau's death, when Miss Tita's sole possession of the papers forces him at last to face the truth of what she feels for him. (James is a master at showing the gradual awakening of a character to a feeling in himself or another which it doesn't suit him to recognise.) He has to face the truth when she gives him the portrait of Jeffrey Aspern. James makes dramatic use of the portrait itself:

> 'You are very generous.'
> 'So are you.'
> 'I don't know why you should think so,' I replied, and this was a truthful speech, for the singular creature seemed to have some very fine reference in her mind, which I did not in the least seize.
> 'Well, you have made a great difference for me,' said Miss Tita.
> I looked at Jeffrey Aspern's face in the little picture, partly in order not to look at that of my interlocutress, which had begun to trouble me, even to frighten me a little—it was so self-conscious, so unnatural. I made no answer to this last declaration; I only privately consulted Jeffrey Aspern's delightful eyes with my own (they were so young and brilliant, and yet so wise, so full of vision); I asked him what on earth was the matter with Miss Tita. He seemed to

> smile at me with friendly mockery, as if he were amused at my case.
> I had got into a pickle for him—as if he needed it! He was unsatis-
> factory, for the only moment since I had known him.   Ch. 9

The narrator finds Aspern unsatisfactory because the situation
demands that he step out of his inveterate role of editor, passive
appreciator and connoisseur and involve himself in life. The
scene, finely focused by the image of the portrait, defines a limit
of the relation between art and life. The papers still belong to life.
He apprehends the vanity of his whole exploit ('I had got into a
pickle for him—as if he needed it!') and then, as she goes on to
make it clear that he can have the papers if he will marry her,
the peculiar poetic justice of his predicament comes home: the
papers are love-letters, and he may possess them only by himself
becoming a lover. This he is not prepared for, so he is left with the
portrait, which belongs to art and is a just reward for his exertions. It may hang appropriately in his temple. Of course he is
not satisfied. He spends the day tormented by his failure and
returns to Miss Tita in the morning, hoping to find some other
way to possess the papers than possessing their guardian, only to
learn that she has accepted her failure and burnt them. The story
ends:

> When, later, I sent her in exchange for the portrait of Jeffrey Aspern
> a larger sum of money than I had hoped to be able to gather for
> her, writing to her that I had sold the picture, she kept it with
> thanks; she never sent it back. I wrote to her that I had sold the
> picture, but . . . it hangs above my writing-table. When I look at it
> my chagrin at the loss of the letters becomes almost intolerable.

Revising the story for the New York Edition twenty years later,
James rewrote the last sentence: 'When I look at it I can scarcely
bear my loss—I mean of the precious papers.' What he had also
lost was Miss Tita, and the revised ending introduces a fine comic
equivocation. It pinpoints the narrator's understanding of his
case: all along he has been more aware of the full truth of it than
it has been comfortable to recognise, and James has created a
narrative style that allows this awareness to peep through without
disturbing the complacent urbanity of its surface. There is a per-

fect balance between vision and blindness. (Of the numerous small alterations James made in revision, about half a dozen in the second half of the text make the narrator more sharply critical of his own behaviour. The rest are stylistic, but well worth studying. My quotations are from the text of 1888.)

Appropriately, Miss Bordereau remains a mysterious figure to the end, it being open to doubt whether her niece fully understands her intentions. It is enough that her tone cuts sharply across the narrator's, asserting a stronger will than his, though in a weaker frame. He deplores her cupidity as 'a false note in my image of the woman who had inspired a great poet with immortal lines', but though he doesn't grudge the gold she extorts from him, and even blames himself for putting her up to the idea of making money, he fails to recognise a similar cupidity in himself, for a different object. Her brutal frankness, so different from the voice he would like to hear coming out of such a past, is a constant reminder of how romantically false his own image of that past is.

Miss Tita emerges more clearly than her aunt as a character with a destiny. A strong contrast with the other two characters was desirable. Apparently 'incapable of grasping more than one clause in any proposition', yet wise in her simplicity; not resenting her seclusion, yet ready to begin life at fifty; and then having the 'force of soul' to accept her failure and 'to smile at me in her humiliation'—she is one of a number of fine portraits in James's work (one thinks of Catherine Sloper in *Washington Square*) of the humble and the oppressed who turn out to have unexpected reserves of moral strength and intelligence. As elsewhere in James, the moral victory is with those who are betrayed and can renounce with a good grace.

The tale is deservedly famous for its setting. The anecdote which gave James his subject—he recounts it in the Preface, and more fully in his Notebook—was set in Florence. He certainly made the most of shifting the scene of it to Venice. The atmosphere of the city is suited to the story of a survival from 'a palpable imaginable visitable past'. Among many admirable passages, there is one in the last chapter which evokes the sociable and domestic character of the Venetian scene, and points out how the transposition of domestic effects to the open air recalls the stage:

> And somehow the splendid common domicile, familiar, domestic and resonant, also resembles a theatre, with actors clicking over bridges and, in straggling processions, tripping along fondamentas. As you sit in your gondola the footways that in certain parts edge the canals assume to the eye the importance of a stage, meeting it at the same angle, and the Venetian figures, moving to and fro against the battered scenery of their little houses of comedy, strike you as members of an endless dramatic troupe.

This is the world of the *commedia dell' arte* and the plays of Goldoni, which end conventionally in a marriage, and its evocation casts an ironic light on the very different ending of James's comedy, in which the self-confessed failure is not redeemed by any conventional tidying-up.

'THE JOLLY CORNER' (1908)

Spencer Brydon, hero of 'The Jolly Corner', is a middle-aged American, returning to New York after some thirty years in Europe. He is a man of leisure, his income based on family property, two houses whose increasing value is one aspect of the thriving American capitalism which has changed the face of the city in his absence. He views this change with some dismay. With the increasing scale of everything, it seems, there go a loss of proportion and an increasing vulgarity:

> Proportions and values were upside-down; the ugly things he had expected, the ugly things of his far-away youth, when he had too promptly waked up to a sense of the ugly—these uncanny phenomena placed him rather, as it happened, under the charm; whereas the 'swagger' things, the modern, the monstrous, the famous things, those he had more particularly, like thousands of ingenuous inquirers every year, come over to see, were exactly his sources of dismay.
>
> Ch. I

Here James sounds a note often heard in his late works: Brydon is one of many characters through whom he expressed his increasing dismay at the way things were going in the world of modern capitalism. Whereas in his earlier works the characters are mainly unaware of, or at least unconcerned about, what their wealth is based on, in the late unfinished novel *The Ivory Tower*, for example, it has become a central concern and a matter of agonised appraisal. In 'The Jolly Corner' it is subsumed under the larger theme of the wanderer returning home, like Ulysses, in a mood of piety, to be confronted by desecration.

Brydon turns for support to an old friend, Alice Staverton. Not enriched, as he has been, by the very process of desecration, she has survived by a delicate frugality. Though not Brydon's wife, in her piety she might recall Penelope, preserving her integrity in his absence and under conditions of siege:

> She stood off, in the awful modern crush, when she could, but she sallied forth and did battle when the challenge was really to 'spirit', the spirit she after all confessed to, proudly and a little shyly, as to that of the better time, that of *their* common, their quite far-away and antediluvian social period and order.   Ch. I

The order in question is not, as in Shakespeare, backed by a coherent structure of generally recognised philosophical ideas and religious beliefs; it's a vague, tenuous, nostalgic concept, and in Brydon it is 'overlaid . . . by the experience of a man and the freedom of a wanderer, overlaid by pleasure, by infidelity, by passages of life that were strange and dim to her, just by "Europe" in short . . .'

With her he visits his properties, both the new one that's going up, where he discovers an unsuspected talent for the practical details of construction and she gently chafes him that 'If he had but stayed at home he would have anticipated the inventor of the skyscraper', and the old one on the 'jolly corner', which for him is a 'consecrated spot'—consecrated by his memory of the family life it has sheltered.

Meanwhile, in a characteristically oblique manner, James has begun to lay the foundations of the psychological drama that is to fill the long central section of the story. 'If he had but stayed at home', says Miss Staverton, 'he would have discovered his genius in time . . .' 'He was to remember these words while the weeks elapsed, for the small silver ring they had sounded over the queerest and deepest of his own lately most disguised and muffled vibrations.' After several pages these 'muffled vibrations', encouraged by the 'ineffaceable life' which the memory of the dead gives to the great empty house, crystallise into the explicit question of 'what he personally might have been, how he might have led his life and "turned out", if he had not so, at the outset, given it up' by going off to live in Europe. Prompted by this question, Brydon begins secretly at night to let himself into the house and prowl there, in search of his *alter ego*, 'some quite erect confronting presence, something planted in the middle of the place and facing him through the dusk'.

The scene is now set, but before the drama begins, he has a conversation with Alice Staverton which adumbrates the very end of the story. She allows the interest of his question about what he might have been, but while he begins to be obsessed with it and fears that 'it must have come to you again and again . . . that I was leading, at any time these thirty years, a selfish frivolous scandalous life', she keeps it calmly in its place:

> 'The great thing to see,' she presently said, 'seems to me to be that it has spoiled nothing. It hasn't spoiled your being here at last. It hasn't spoiled this. It hasn't spoiled your speaking—' She also however faltered.
>
> He wondered at everything her controlled emotion might mean. 'Do you believe then—too dreadfully!—that I *am* as good as I might ever have been?'
>
> 'Oh no! Far from it!' With which she got up from her chair and was nearer to him. 'But I don't care,' she smiled.
>
> 'You mean I'm good enough?'
>
> She considered a little. 'Will you believe it if I say so? I mean will you let that settle your question for you?'   Ch. 1

In other words, she's saying: 'Give up this morbid obsession and take what life still has to offer—take me!' But he can't, yet: 'he drew back from this'. She recognises, as he does, that things might have been otherwise, possibly better, but she keeps the past and the possible in their place. Her attitude is the sane one of acceptance and a patient tranquillity. Uprooted and still wandering, he is too restless, disturbed and self-absorbed to adopt it, and so falls prey to his obsession.

In the second section of the story, in which he tracks his prey, his other self, and brings him to bay, we enter fully into Brydon's view of the case. This doesn't mean we are to share it uncritically. The first section has introduced the main themes, given us Alice Staverton's calmer, more detached view of Brydon's quest, and anticipated its resolution, and we bear this in mind as we watch him prowl. We share his excitement and terror, and these are finely evoked. The greater part of the story is the narrative of the chase, brought alive in a wealth of descriptive detail. But it would be wrong to suppose that James is going all out to terrify the reader. As in 'The Turn of the Screw', any such crude intention is belied both by what has gone before and by the elegance, humour and moderation of the writing. These qualities of James's late style express his hero's fine consciousness, the elegance of mind and the good humour that do not desert him in the heat of action. Mere abject terror Brydon resists as shameful, and James could arouse it in the reader only by an elaborate mysteriousness of incident, a mystification that he never attempts. The incidents of the chase are few and simple; what makes it rich is the range of possibilities to which the situation gives rise in the hero's mind, as he cultivates his 'whole perception':

> He projected himself all day, in thought, straight over the bristling line of hard unconscious heads and into the other, the real, the waiting life; the life that, as soon as he had heard behind him the click of his great house-door, began for him, on the jolly corner, as beguilingly as the slow opening bars of some rich music follows the tap of the conductor's wand.   Ch. 2

The crisis comes, one night, with his finding a door closed at the top of the house which he reckons to have left open only a short time before. His prey must have taken refuge behind it. Faced with this undoubted sign of the other's presence, he hesitates between courageous attack and terrified flight, until 'insistence' gives way to 'discretion': he will merely stand by the closed door a little to assert his own answering presence, and then 'spare' the stranger by a dignified withdrawal. He begins the long descent to the ground floor, down the staircase whose well is imaged as 'some watery underworld' and where the marble squares that pave the hall below figure 'the bottom of the sea'. But before he reaches the bottom he is faced with the second manifestation of 'some inconceivable occult activity': not a closed door this time, but an open one, beyond which the hunted stranger at last visibly stands.

What follows is both exciting and convincing, but not at all easy to explain. It may be suggested that what Brydon has been in search of is confirmation of his own identity. In the thoroughly changed America to which he has returned, what he has lived for finds no recognition. If by never going away he might really have been quite different, this throws doubt on what he is, and he is threatened by a possible void, a negation of his personality, a kind of death of the spirit. His anxiety focuses on the idea of an *alter ego*; he feels he must confront it and know the worst before he can be himself again. When 'the other' merely stands there with his face covered, 'buried as for dark deprecation', Brydon takes it 'as a proof that *he*, standing there for the achieved, the enjoyed, the triumphant life, couldn't be faced in his triumph'. So for a moment Brydon is able to preserve the illusion of his own self-sufficiency: he went to Europe to 'live', and though it may have seemed 'a selfish frivolous scandalous life' in the eyes of some, perhaps after all it was justified:

> Wasn't the proof in the splendid covering hands, strong and completely spread?—so spread and so intentional that, in spite of a special verity that surpassed every other, the fact that one of the hands had lost two fingers, which were reduced to stumps, as if accidentally shot away, the face was effectually guarded and saved.
>
> Ch. 2

The maimed hand represents a fact about 'the other's' American life: in contrast to Brydon's in Europe, it has been one of physical and aesthetic deprivation. But the next moment 'the other' drops his hands and advances upon Brydon with face disclosed, and now it is Brydon who fails. He cannot accept this other self, the face proves 'too horrible' for recognition:

> The bared identity was too hideous as his ... The face, *that* face, Spencer Brydon's?—he searched it still, but looking away from it in dismay and denial, falling straight from his height of sublimity. It was unknown, inconceivable, awful, disconnected from any possibility ... Such an identity fitted his at *no* point, made its alternative monstrous. A thousand times yes, as it came upon him nearer now—the face was the face of a stranger.   Ch. 2

It becomes clear in the last section of the story that this denial of Brydon's is a kind of failure of the imagination, or of charity. It is in any case a failure of personality or identity:

> ... and falling back as under the hot breath and the roused passion of a life larger than his own, a rage of personality before which his own collapsed, he felt the whole vision turn to darkness and his very feet give way. His head went round; he was going; he had gone.
>   Ch. 2

The conclusion is in a way very simple. He is found later that day at the foot of the stairs,

> as he appeared to have fallen, but all so wondrously without bruise or gash, only in a depth of stupor. What he most took in, however, at present, with the steadier clearance, was that Alice Staverton had for a long unspeakable moment not doubted he was dead.
>
> 'It must have been that I *was*.' He made it out as she held him. 'Yes—I can only have died. You brought me literally to life. Only,' he wondered, his eyes rising to her, 'only, in the name of all the benedictions, how?'
>
> It took her but an instant to bend her face and kiss him, and something in the manner of it, and in the way her hands clasped and locked his head while he felt the cool charity and virtue of her lips, something in all this beatitude somehow answered everything. 'And now I keep you,' she said.   Ch. 3

He has been brought to life by the saving power of her love. (The language is notably religious.) Their last conversation supplies a commentary on what has occurred. Alice Staverton has waited for him patiently all these years. He has not recognised her love, but now he can and must accept it. And her love is only efficacious and redemptive because, having seen the other, the 'black stranger', more than once in a dream and again this very morning, she has accepted him and pitied him:

> 'I *could* have liked him. And to me,' she said, 'he was no horror. I had accepted him.'
> ' "Accepted"—?' Brydon oddly sounded.
> 'Before, for the interest of his difference—yes. And as *I* didn't disown him, as *I* knew him—which you at last, confronted with him in his difference, so cruelly didn't, my dear—well, he must have been, you see, less dreadful to me. And it may have pleased him that I pitied him.'   Ch. 3

They argue about his identity, and Brydon rejects any connection with himself, while she quietly insists on the relevance and value of 'the other', for all his difference. He has brought them together. Brydon has all his fingers, and a 'charming monocle' instead of the other's 'great convex pince-nez', but the vision of each, in his different way, has been impaired. She makes the comparison as though to say that either way, by staying in America to make money or by going to Europe to spend it, Brydon must have blindly, by selfishness, missed the greatest good of all. However, she allows him, the weaker vessel, to cling to the idea which the reader, with her, now sees to be a quibble:

> 'And he isn't—no, he isn't—*you!*' she murmured as he drew her to his breast.

It needs to be emphasised with what delicacy ideas are suggested to the reader which the critic, trying to answer the question 'What is the story about?' by abstracting them from their context, can only formulate with relative crudity. Superficially, the tale belongs to the popular tradition of the ghost story, but James transcends that tradition, both by his psychological penetration of the way obsession may work in the most refined and intelligent consciousness, and by raising deep questions about the life and death of the spirit without abandoning a modern setting and a realistic plot.

8

Summary and Conclusion

Difficulty. James is harder to read than any great novelist before him, and the difficulty increases in the later works. There are at least two reasons for this. Earlier novelists tended to explain their characters and the action directly to the reader, from a position of detached omniscience. Writing less and less from such a position, James makes the reader share the characters' perplexities. Secondly, his characters are constantly making distinctions, chiefly moral distinctions, more subtle than other writers attempt. The difficulty is *not* a merely stylistic matter: the late style is functional, determined by what James is doing. When a French translator told him that his late work was proving untranslatable, James was delighted and said this showed 'that in a literary work of the least complexity the very form and texture are the substance itself and that the flesh is indetachable from the bones'.

Point of view. Consciously and deliberately, James restricted himself more and more to narrating from the point of view of his principal characters. He saw this as realistic: the author effaces himself and the reader gets close to the subject. The subject is not what happens but what the characters think and feel about what happens, and this experience of theirs, rather than any generalisations the author might make upon it, is the centre of interest. Another reason for thus limiting the narrative point of view was that it made for a satisfactory coherence and integrity. Influenced more by French theory and example than by English, James wanted his novels to be coherent and shapely works of art. He deplored the tendency of most novelists to let their subjects sprawl out: life might be untidy, but art should not be. 'Fluid puddings' and 'loose baggy monsters' was what he called the novels of Tolstoy and Dostoevsky, with their 'promiscuous shiftings of standpoint and centre'. He saw that this was 'the inevitable result of the *quantity of presenting* their genius launches them in. With the complexity they pile up they *can* get no clearness without trying again and again for new centres.' He preferred to limit his 'centre' or narrative point of view, even if this meant limiting the amount of material that could be presented.

'Dramatise, dramatise!' Narration from a character's point of view is balanced by what James called the *scene*, in which the words and actions of his characters are reported and shown directly, with a minimum of authorial intrusion. This was another way for the author to efface himself. To have plenty of *scenes*, which are dramatic and 'objective', compensates for the subjectivity of restricting the narrative passages to the characters' point of view.

Omissions. The subject of his novels is a certain action, unique in the lives of those involved, and only what belongs to that action should be included. It follows that James's work has no room for showing men and women involved in the characteristic activities of everyday life. Giving birth and dying, physical labour, eating and drinking, travelling, 'management of men', the life of institutions, all kinds of work and play—everything in life that's *habitual* finds no place in his work. In this respect his novels are more like a play by Racine than a novel by Dickens or Tolstoy.

Society. James's characters, especially in the later works, may therefore seem to exist in a social vacuum. This effect is increased by their usually being wealthy, and thus independent of a daily routine. (When his heroes and heroines are poor and confined by their material needs, as the hero of *The Princess Casamassima* is tied to his bookbinding, or the heroine of 'In the Cage' to her telegraphist's office, their confinement is emphasised only to show how they transcend it by their 'range of wonderment', their 'winged intelligence'.) Furthermore, the wealthy tend to be rootless. They don't usually have a clearly defined social position and function. This reflects James's own experience, but also a tendency of the age: the populations of Britain and the United States more than doubled in James's lifetime, millions migrated from the country to the cities, and old social patterns were broken up. His work doesn't show this happening as a large social process, but the way his characters live—meeting and dispersing, meeting again in another place, their contacts sporadic and with long gaps of time between—reflects realistically the opportunities and deprivations of the rich in that period of social dislocation.

The physical and aesthetic aspects of social life were real to James. The way people dress, move about, enter or leave a room, group themselves, their gestures and expressions and tones of voice in conversation—his imaginative grasp of these details animates the scenes in his fiction, giving them some of the 'body', the substantiality of drama on the stage.

Dialogue. James was quite capable of rendering people's different ways of talking in a realistic manner; but more and more, in the later works, the characters talk a special Jamesian language. This is frankly unrealistic. If they didn't use this language there would be a stylistic gap between dialogue and narrative. In most novelists such a gap doesn't matter: they don't aspire to give a consistent texture to the whole work, both dialogue and narrative. James did aspire to this. As he came, in narrative passages, to render with greater subtlety the complex web of experience of his characters at certain carefully selected moments of their lives, so his narrative style grew more complicated and idiosyncratic. The dialogue grows more stylised to match it. This style could be said to express the exceptional sensibility of the characters, enabling them to make the same sort of subtle discriminations as are made in the narrative. But since the same style is also used by stupid or vulgar characters, one must suppose that it seemed more important to James that the work as a whole should maintain a certain level of style than that his characters should display a realistic variation of idiom. Similar conventions govern most of the world's great drama.

'*Mixture of manners*'. James had a special eye for the ways in which manners express the intellectual and moral life of classes, societies and peoples. Increasing mobility was breaking down old barriers, and James was well placed, by upbringing, to be the first writer to exhibit the consequent 'mixture of manners', as between Europe and America, in a great variety of situations and with cosmopolitan detachment. At a superficial level new contacts across national boundaries, especially between the sexes, produced a rich crop of those perplexities, misunderstandings, embarrassments, snags and hitches that have always been the staple of comedy. But the lightest of his international fictions reflect serious issues, and in some of his major works an international situation becomes the context for a tragic drama.

Places. James had a strong feeling for the character of places. Rooms, houses, gardens, streets, cities, the time of day and year—these circumstances come alive in his fiction not by means of methodical, objective description, but subjectively, as they affect the characters and combine with their other experience of the moment. Some of his characters have his own appreciation of the urban scene. They regard cities not as centres of power or realms to be conquered, as do the heroes of Balzac and Stendhal, but as works of art and expressions of civilisation to which one must submit and respond; they are to be possessed only by the imagination. (See especially *Roderick Hudson* and *The Princess Casamassima*.)

Freedom and necessity. In earlier novelists the limits of freedom are less vague than in James. If a happy ending is in question at all, there tends to be no doubt about the terms on which the good life may be lived and happiness be won. For James's characters, wealthy and socially adrift, the question of freedom and necessity arises in a peculiarly uncertain form.

Moral choice. Together with this uncertainty about what they *can* do, goes a peculiar uncertainty about what they *ought* to do. Their decisive moral choices are made in isolation from the circumstances that would condition such choices in real life. This may be illustrated by comparing the similar dilemmas of Maggie Tulliver, heroine of George Eliot's *The Mill on the Floss* (1860), and Fleda Vetch, heroine of James's short novel *The Spoils of Poynton* (1897). Each decides she must give up the man she loves so that he may honour a previous engagement to another girl, but in *The Mill on the Floss* the arguments for renunciation are much stronger: as well as Stephen's engagement to Lucy there is Maggie's to Philip, and neither Lucy nor Philip, unlike James's Mona, has behaved unworthily. There is also the social community, the whole way of life which we have watched Maggie growing up in and learning to love—this too would be denied if she gave in to her present passion (see Bk. 6, Ch. 14). In James there is none of this: the characters have no background to speak of ('her meagre past fell away from her like a garment of the wrong fashion'), and there is no depicted social or religious structure that claims their allegiance and embodies the principles they live by. Fleda's moral struggle therefore takes place in a comparative vacuum. Her sacrifice is made less for Mona's sake than for that of her own self-esteem, her own and her lover's 'common honour'. She cannot respect him unless he honours his engagement, and she cannot respect herself unless she helps him to do so. The fact that this may frustrate their love for each other and make their lives a misery doesn't affect the heroism of a 'high and delicate deed' (Ch. 9).

If James's characters are remarkably free from conditioning factors, the virtuous ones manage nevertheless to make things pretty hard for themselves, and their drama frequently ends in renunciation—in Fleda's words, 'something dreamed and missed, something reduced, relinquished, resigned: the poetry, as it were, of something sensibly *gone*'. James seems to have had an extraordinary feeling both for how free from external necessities life might ideally be, and for the elaborate constraints that an ideally scrupulous conscience would impose upon itself.

General ideas. T. S. Eliot said of James, 'He had a mind so fine that no idea could violate it'. Presumably he meant, not that James's mind never entertained any general ideas, but that as an artist he kept them in their proper place, subordinate to the particular situation in which they arise. This is one aspect of James's self-effacement as a writer. Like Jane Austen and unlike many of his contemporaries, he doesn't preach to the reader or moralise explicitly. This doesn't mean that he thought literature had nothing to do with general ideas or with morality. He once said no fiction was 'worth its salt' if it didn't contain any general ideas. They are constantly implicit in the reflections of his characters on their experience, and they abound in his other writing—letters, criticism, travel books, the New York Prefaces and the autobiography. As for the relation of art to morality, James can have the last word:

> There is, I think, no more nutritive or suggestive truth in this connexion than that of the perfect dependence of the 'moral' sense of a work of art on the amount of felt life concerned in producing it.
> Preface to THE PORTRAIT OF A LADY

James had a very long working life. The size, range and consistently high standard of his *œuvre* make it the most impressive monument in the history of English and American literature to a writer's devotion to his craft. If you want to criticise him, you have to compare him to the very greatest. You can say that he hasn't Tolstoy's comprehensive vision of the life of body and mind and soul as all one life, or the solid social specification of Stendhal or George Eliot, placing their characters firmly in a densely realised social world which they are nevertheless seen to be able to transcend. As a novelist, he doesn't command that variety of genre, convention and style that Shakespeare covers as he moves from comedy to history to tragedy, both between plays and within them. Still, for a novelist he covered a wide range of comic and tragic effects, and developed a style that could sound tragic notes under a witty comic surface. He brought to the writing of fiction standards of craftsmanship, especially in the development of plot, that make most novelists look hopelessly untidy. He dramatised moral problems with unique subtlety. Above all, without resort to caricature he reacted an extraordinary number of memorable characters, men and women, who will keep you company long after you have closed his pages.

Select Bibliography

NOVELS

Dates indicate the first publication in book form, which was preceded in most cases by serialisation in a magazine. P = currently published by Penguin. BH = currently published by The Bodley Head.

Watch and Ward (1878)
Roderick Hudson (1875)
The American (1877)
The Europeans (1878) P, BH
Confidence (1879)
Washington Square (1880) P, BH
The Portrait of a Lady (1881) P, BH
The Bostonians (1886) P, BH
The Princess Casamassima (1886) BH
The Reverberator (1888)
The Tragic Muse (1890)
The Other House (1896)
The Spoils of Poynton (1897) P, BH
What Maisie Knew (1897) P, BH
The Awkward Age (1899) P, BH
The Sacred Fount (1901)
The Ambassadors (1903) BH
The Wings of the Dove (1902) P, BH
The Golden Bowl (1904) P, BH
The Outcry (1911)
The Ivory Tower, unfinished (1917)
The Sense of the Past, unfinished (1917)

TALES

The Complete Tales of Henry James, ed. Leon Edel. 12 vols.
(Rupert Hart-Davis, 1962–4).
Various one-volume selections are available.

OTHER WORKS

The Complete Plays of Henry James, ed. Leon Edel (1949).
Henry James: Autobiography, ed. F. W. Dupee (1956). This collects
in one volume the three autobiographical works *A Small Boy
and Others* (1913), *Notes of a Son and Brother* (1914) and the
unfinished *Middle Years* (1917).
The American Scene (1907) (Rupert Hart-Davis, 1968).
The House of Fiction, essays on the novel by Henry James, ed.
Leon Edel (Rupert Hart-Davis, 1957).
Henry James: Selected Literary Criticism, ed. Morris Shapira (Pen-
guin, 1968).
The Art of the Novel. Critical Prefaces by Henry James, ed. R. P.
Blackmur (Scribners, 1934). This collects in one volume all the
prefaces James wrote for the New York Edition of his works,
1907–9.
The Notebooks of Henry James, eds. F. O. Matthiessen and Kenneth
B. Murdock (Oxford, 1947).
Selected Letters of Henry James, ed. Leon Edel (Rupert Hart-Davis,
1956).

BIOGRAPHY

The Life of Henry James, by Leon Edel, in 5 vols: *The Untried
Years, 1843–70*; *The Conquest of London, 1870–83*; *The Middle
Years, 1883–94*; *The Treacherous Years, 1895–1900*; *The Master,
1901–16* (Rupert Hart-Davis, 1953–72).

CRITICISM

Henry James, by D. W. Jefferson, in the series 'Writers and
Critics' (Oliver and Boyd, 1960).

Henry James, the Major Phase, by F. O. Matthiessen (Oxford, 1963). This deals with the late novels, from *The Ambassadors* onwards.

Eight Modern Writers, by J. I. M. Stewart (Oxford, 1963). Contains a long chapter on James and a full bibliography.

The Great Tradition: George Eliot, Henry James, Joseph Conrad, by F. R. Leavis (Chatto and Windus, 1960).

An Introduction to the English Novel, by Arnold Kettle (Hutchinson, 1953). Vol. 2 has a chapter on *The Portrait of a Lady*.

The Triple Thinkers, by Edmund Wilson (Penguin, 1963). Contains an essay on 'The Ambiguity of Henry James'.

Index to the Works of Henry James

General Index